I Ching

I Ching

Navigate life's transitions
using ancient oracles
of the I Ching

Antonia and Bill Beattie

BARNES
& NOBLE
BOOKS
NEW YORK

Contents

Introduction

What is the I Ching?

The I Ching (pronounced 'eye cheeng' or 'ee cheeng'), or Book of Changes as it is also known, is a book of divination. It is perhaps the oldest philosophical writing in Chinese civilization, and its wisdom provides the bases for such practices as Chinese medicine, Chinese astrology, feng shui and tai chi. It offers a key to many areas of our lives.

The concepts of the I Ching, first conceived by legendary Chinese emperor and sage Fu Hsi, have provided advice for over 3000 years. The early emperors of China, living in troubled times, were the first to use the wisdom of the I Ching. Later the work became generally available, helping people from all walks of life.

The I Ching is the essence of **Taoist philosophy***. This is one of the great philosophies of China. It includes the notion of 'oneness,' and the view that everything in the universe is part of an ongoing cycle. The natural forces and the human world are interlinked. Our relationships and our circumstances mirror the flow of changes in the natural world.

The I Ching is an orderly system, based on observations of the natural forces. It explains the patterns and rhythms of the energy that flows in nature. Consulting it also enables us to understand the patterns and rhythms of our own existence.

For many years, the I Ching has provided practical and rational help in times of turmoil and chaos. Let the wisdom of the I Ching bring order and understanding into your life.

The Energy in everything

In Chinese philosophy, it is believed that a strong life force, called '**qi**' '**chi**,' or '**ki**,' flows around and within every object and living thing. It is generated by the interaction between two opposing forces, the two primal forces of nature. These are known as '**yin**,' feminine, and '**yang**,' masculine, energy. Both forms of energy are necessary for life to survive; neither is better than the other. Chinese philosophy describes the flow of nature and the progress of life as the constant balancing and rebalancing of yin and yang energy.

---

* All terms in bold appear in the Glossary.

Yin and yang

In the I Ching, and Chinese philosophy generally, the feminine or 'yin' energy came to be symbolized by a short, broken line, representing a yielding form of energy. Correspondingly, a short unbroken line indicates masculine or 'yang' energy, a forceful form of energy.

yang   *yin*

Yang	Yin
Solid line	Broken line
Heaven	Earth
Masculine principle	Feminine principle
Activity	Passivity
Movement	Stillness
Heat	Cold
Full energy	Hidden potential energy
Exterior	Interior

Combining yin and yang

It was believed that after the Ultimate Beginning of the universe the two primary powers of yin and yang interacted. Four different energy combinations were produced. Each was represented as a stack of two lines, broken for yin and solid for yang. The top line represented Heaven and the bottom Earth. Later a center line was added to each to represent humanity, poised between Heaven and Earth. These three lines represent the **san cai** or the trinity of cosmic unity between Heaven, Earth and humanity.

heaven

humanity

earth

The trigrams

The three-line figure comprising yin and/or yang lines is the basic unit of meaning of the I Ching. It is known as a **trigram**, and there are eight in total, formed from all possible combinations of yin and yang lines. Each trigram is associated with one of eight natural forces of nature: Heaven, Earth, Thunder, Wind, Water, Fire, Mountain or Lake.

Consistent with the Chinese belief that everything is interrelated, each trigram also indicates various aspects of life, not only the energy form of a force of nature. It has a symbolic meaning and depicts physical, psychological, natural and social manifestations (see the table opposite).

The position of each line in a trigram also represents a particular aspect of nature and our lives. The top line corresponds with Heaven and cosmological energies, and relates to our spiritual or mental condition. The bottom line represents Earth and our personal issues, such as money and health. The middle line corresponds with humanity, culture and politics, as well as our emotional and psychological condition.

The most predominantly yang trigram (Heaven) is represented as the "Father," and the most predominantly yin (Earth,) as the "Mother." The remaining trigrams are assigned to first, second and third "Sons" and "Daughters" (see opposite).

The hexagrams

In the I Ching, each of the eight trigrams is paired with another trigram, forming 64 **hexagrams**, or six-line figures. The top trigram represents what is happening in the celestial world, beyond our power, while the bottom trigram indicates what is happening in our world, within our control. The commentary on the 64 hexagrams forms the text of the I Ching. Each hexagram represents a standard situation that has occurred regularly through-out human history. The combination of six yin and/or yang lines indicates the levels of yin and yang energy present in the particular situation. The hexagrams symbolize the full scope of human interaction, and the relationship between humans and the universe.

Heaven (Qian)
• Yang
• Father
• Creative energy
• Virtue, health, perseverance, power, charity, dignity, prosperity, originality, the higher self, protection

Thunder (Chen)
• Yang
• First Son
• High energy
• Agitation, impetus, vigor, confrontation, renewal, imminent revolutions

Water (Kan)
• Yang
• Second Son
• Adaptive energy
• Vitality, adventures, concealment, fluidity, cruelty, hard work, dormancy, uncertainty, perils

Mountain (Ken)
• Yang
• Third Son
• Revolutionary
• Energy
• Accomplishment, faithfulness, retreat, world philosophies stubbornness, deep thinking, thriftiness, stagnation

Earth (Kun)
• Yin
• Mother
• Receptive energy
• Elegance, passivity, devotion, dependability, fertility, maturity, mildness, security, vulnerability, kindness

Wind (Xun)
• Yin
• First Daughter
• Penetrating energy
• Romance, lying, pervasiveness, growth, transformation, courtesy, fleetingness, affection

Fire (Li)
• Yin
• Second Daughter
• Illuminative energy
• Passion, extremes, insight, awareness, uniqueness, talent, discrimination, dependency, charisma, volatility, celebrations, immortals

Lake (Dui)
• Yin
• Third Daughter
• Joyous energy
• Gracefulness, serenity, tranquillity, sensuality, talkativeness, narcissism, gaiety

Consulting the I Ching

To seek enlightenment from the wisdom of the I Ching, you will need to be in a relaxed state of mind, free of the clutter of thoughts and anxieties. Do stretching or breathing exercises, or take time to meditate and release all your worries. Allow your mind to feel clear so that you can receive the full benefit of the wisdom of the I Ching. Then do the following.

Asking a question

Ask the I Ching only one question at a time, and make sure it is not too complex. Ask only about issues that really matter to you, such as health, financial matters, social situations, business decisions or what to expect if you travel or enter into a particular venture. Do not ask trivial questions out of curiosity. The I Ching works best when you are in earnest to find out about your situation, and ask from the heart.

Using coins to 'cast' for a reply

There are many ways to consult the I Ching. With the simplest method, given here, you can use a coin. For other methods, see 'Further Reading,' page 79.

Take the coin in your left hand. One side (traditionally heads) is 'yang;' the other (traditionally tails) is 'yin.' State your question out loud and throw the coin. If your throw produces heads (yang), draw a short unbroken line. For tails (yin), draw a short broken line.

Constructing a six-line figure: your key hexagram

Continue to think of your question. Toss your coin again and draw the resultant broken or unbroken line above your first line. Do this six times in total, adding to the top of the stack. The six-line figure will form one of the 64 I Ching hexagrams and will represent the I Ching's answer to your question.

Finding your hexagram in the I Ching

To identify the number of the hexagram, divide it into two trigrams—the top three lines form the upper trigram, and the bottom three lines the lower trigram.

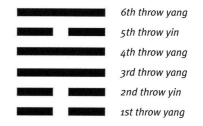

6th throw yang

5th throw yin

4th throw yang

3rd throw yang

2nd throw yin

1st throw yang

Identifying your hexagram

In the table, find your top trigram in the upper horizontal line. Now find your lower trigram in the vertical line of the table. Trace a line down from the top trigram to the lower one you have identified. Where the lines meet you will find a replica of your hexagram, and its number.

Reading the message

Hexagrams 1–64 are described, in order, from pages 14 to 77. Find your hexagram and read its message. Apply this to the question with which you began your coin throwing.

▶ UPPER TRIGRAM / ▼ LOWER TRIGRAM	HEAVEN	EARTH	THUNDER	WIND	WATER	FIRE	MOUNTAIN	LAKE
HEAVEN	1 Ch'ien page 12	11 T'ai page 22	34 Ta Chuang page 45	9 Hsiao Ch'u page 20	5 Hsu page 16	14 Ta Yu page 25	26 Ta Ch'u page 37	43 Kuai page 54
EARTH	12 P'i page 23	2 K'un page 13	16 Yu page 27	20 Kuan page 31	8 Pi page 19	35 Chin page 46	23 Po page 34	45 Ts'ui page 56
THUNDER	25 Wu Wang page 36	24 Fu page 35	51 Chen page 62	42 I page 53	3 Chun page 14	21 Shih Ho page 32	27 I page 38	17 Sui page 28
WIND	44 Kou page 55	46 Sheng page 57	32 Heng page 43	57 Sun page 68	48 Ching page 59	50 Ting page 61	18 Ku page 29	28 Ta Kuo page 39
WATER	6 Sung page 17	7 Shih page 18	40 Hsieh page 51	59 Huan page 70	29 K'an page 40	64 Wei Chi page 75	4 Meng page 15	47 K'un page 58
FIRE	13 T'ung Jen page 24	36 Ming I page 47	55 Feng page 66	37 Chia Jen page 48	63 Chi Chi page 74	30 Li page 41	22 Pi page 33	49 Ko page 60
MOUNTAIN	33 Tun page 44	15 Ch'ien page 26	62 Hsaio Kuo page 73	53 Chien page 64	39 Chien page 50	56 Lu page 67	52 Ken page 63	31 Hsien page 42
LAKE	10 Lu page 21	19 Lin page 30	54 Kuei Mei page 65	61 Chung Fu page 72	60 Chieh page 71	38 K'uei page 49	41 Sun page 52	58 Tui page 69

The 64 Hexagrams

Hexagram 1
Ch'ien (The Creative)

Ch'ien is formed by the two trigrams Heaven over Heaven. This is pure yang energy, indicating a time when we are strongly placed to begin achieving our objectives, realizing our dreams and increasing our personal power.

The lack of yin influence is an indication that this creative force has not yet acted, and exists in potential only. The receptivity of yin is required before it can be used. This is therefore a time of preparation and the taking of initial steps.

The I Ching uses the image of an Emperor to represent this sheer yang potency. The Emperor must be open to the influence of powers greater than himself, and must be mindful that to rule is nothing, but to rule well is a triumph. This hexagram advises us that great things may be accomplished, but if they are to have lasting value they must be born of virtuous motivations. It is important to move forward with compassion rather than arrogance, as this will only breed resentment or complacency in those around us.

Ch'ien is highly auspicious, but it signifies beginnings rather than attainment. When filled with yang energy, we may feel the desire to build Rome (or perhaps Beijing) in a day. However, major achievements require the unfaltering commitment and effort advocated by this hexagram. We should not allow impatience to dampen our enthusiasm.

GUIDANCE FROM HEXAGRAM 1	
General	You can realize your potential for achievement through persistent effort and enthusiasm
Love	Try to behave in a compassionate manner toward your partner
Business	Your ideas have merit, but take time to work out a sound strategy so that your schemes will work
Lifestyle	Be kind to yourself and give yourself time to relax and enjoy life

Hexagram 2
K'un (The Receptive)

K'un is formed by two purely yin trigrams—Earth over Earth. This suggests a time when we will benefit from being open, obedient and humble rather than from using force of will to batter down obstacles.

With yang lines absent, K'un emphasizes that this is a period when we will make more progress by following the advice of a respected friend, relation or mentor than by attempting to find our own way forward. The I Ching reminds us that life is in a constant state of flux. Accordingly, the submissiveness of K'un is recommended not as a strategy for life, but only as suitable for this moment. Neither action nor passivity in themselves guarantee success, but knowing when each is appropriate will.

The two Earth trigrams suggest the image of fertile soil. On its own the soil produces nothing, but it absorbs all that is needed to nourish and nurture the seeds that are sown into it. When K'un reflects our situation, we are similarly able to receive the wisdom, ideas and guidance of others and, in time, bring forth a harvest of achievement. If, on the contrary, we willfully refuse to remain open to the influences of others, we will be as unproductive as unseeded earth.

Just as the seed within the Earth or the child within the womb must grow at its own slow, steady rate, so at this time our projects will be unresponsive to attempts to hasten them. Tranquil persistence will bring pleasing results.

GUIDANCE FROM HEXAGRAM 2	
General	Be receptive to the influence of those worthy of respect—this is a sign of strength, not weakness
Love	Heed the advice of your family and friends
Business	Take stock of your situation and listen to industry experts
Lifestyle	Take advice from a counselor or specialist you trust

Hexagram 3
Chun (Problems at the Beginning)

In Chun, the Water trigram is above that of Thunder. The image this evokes is of heavy storm clouds unleashing a downpour over a landscape that echoes with thunder. Although this suggests a period of tribulation and darkness, Chun reminds us that such storms are frequently brief and that the land may benefit from the deeply penetrating rainfall. In its aftermath the air is cleared and new growth is enhanced.

Just as many children are brought safely into the world after a difficult birth, so newly initiated enterprises often need to pass through a period of turmoil and confusion before they are able to flourish. As we undertake new projects, we bear the burden of our inexperience and may at times feel as vulnerable as children caught in a storm. Chun asks us to recognize the inevitability of these trials and to face them with courage, remaining willing to learn from the darkness rather than surrendering at the first sign of hardship.

At the same time we should be wary of reckless action. Before forging ahead, we must learn, discovering order within chaos and separating truth from illusion. Misleading or corrupting influences must be recognized. Alliances made and advice received at this time must be carefully analyzed—the world is filled with those who, often with good intentions, only add to its confusion. Those most at risk in the world are those whose ignorance obscures their awareness of how much they have to learn.

GUIDANCE FROM HEXAGRAM 3	
General	Acknowledgment of inexperience is the first step to learning
Love	You may have reached a stumbling block in your relationship, but it will not last if you learn from the problem
Business	Assess your business dealings and work out how to do business better
Lifestyle	You may have hit a setback, but this will be merely temporary if you make adjustments to your lifestyle

Hexagram 4
Meng (Youthful Folly)

Meng is formed by Mountain over Water, which suggests the flowing of a stream from its source in a mountain spring. The small stream babbles away contentedly as it continues its journey; its bed is shallow and its course easily diverted. It has quite some distance to travel before it becomes a substantial river.

This image develops the theme of inexperience seen in hexagram 3. The rivulet is likened to a young and naive mind. The untutored character has the exuberance and purity of a mountain stream but is not yet equipped to become a force in the world.

Meng instructs us that education must always be a matter of enhancing the student's true nature rather than repressing it. A good teacher looks upon the joy and playfulness of the young not as an inhibitor of learning but as something to channel into the process. When there is pleasure in learning, the young will be drawn to their teachers rather than merely tolerating them.

Ignorance is not a force to be conquered—it is merely an absence. It should not be punished harshly, but should be replaced instead with knowledge passed on with patience and forbearance. The child will learn as much from the manner of the teacher as from the lessons themselves. A well-loved teacher will become a powerful role model, while a careless, impatient instructor is more likely to engender a disrespect for authority that may impede progress. The empty cup of an inexperienced mind must be filled gently.

GUIDANCE FROM HEXAGRAM 4	
General	The keys to both learning and teaching are patience, kindness and consistency
Love	Taking time, gently release childhood traumas about relationships
Business	Strengthen any new business procedures with thoughtfulness
Lifestyle	Tap into the joyfulness and pleasure of youth, and release any bad habits that you may have had since childhood

Hsu (Waiting, Nourishment)

Hsu consists of Water over Heaven. This suggests water vapor rising to the sky to form clouds that will, in time, shower rain onto the thirsty land beneath them. These clouds, heavy with rain that has not yet begun to fall, symbolize all that we require but cannot control. The rain will start, but we are unable to hurry it.

This hexagram therefore relates to waiting and patience, something many of us would rather do without. Both, however, are inescapable parts of life, and Hsu reminds us that there is a world of difference between merely hoping for something, and waiting for a change that we are confident will happen. The longest drought will be broken and the hardest winter will turn to Spring. Enduring such trials is not easy, but the knowledge that they must necessarily end gives us the strength to prevail.

When we find ourselves in these sorts of fallow periods in life, Hsu advises against frittering away energy on worry and premature action. We should instead use the time to prepare ourselves optimally for the opportunities we are anticipating. Our strategies and ambitions should be honed and our bodies and spirits strengthened and nourished.

When we act in accordance with these principles, periods of waiting will never be wasted time. In order to capitalize on the forthcoming upturn in fortune, we should strengthen ourselves instead of being debilitated by doubt.

GUIDANCE FROM HEXAGRAM 5

General	To wait in doubt is a hardship; to wait with confidence is not
Love	If single, you will find your relationship in due time; if you have a partner, you will soon enter a happier period
Business	Set up your business, or continue it, with the confidence that you will succeed
Lifestyle	Work on releasing current worries and anxieties; get some perspective on your life

Hexagram 6
Sung (Conflict)

Sung is formed by the trigrams Heaven over Water. Because water tends to flow to the deepest space available, it distances itself from the heavens as much as possible. As rain falls from the sky and steadily increases its remoteness from the clouds in which it was suspended, so human conflict can be measured by the distance between individuals and their inability to communicate with one another.

When two people, or two nations, make a virtue of being alienated from each other, disaster threatens. It does not matter who is in the right. The antagonism generated by a reluctance to communicate will be damaging to all.

War between two countries exposes the failure of governments; open hostility between individuals reveals the errors of both parties. Sung urges us to take all possible steps to prevent the outbreak of such conflicts and to bridge the gap inhibiting communication. The mediation of a level-headed and impartial third party will frequently be the wisest course.

Sung also recommends that we resolve the conflicts within ourselves, since these often give rise to belligerence toward others. The least tolerant people are typically the ones who suffer most from internal conflicts, such as racists crippled by a fear of the unfamiliar. We need to identify the areas of self-righteousness within ourselves and resolve the fear and confusion they usually mask. Then we will become more capable of avoiding, and preventing the escalation of, disputes of all natures.

GUIDANCE FROM HEXAGRAM 6

General	Hostility increases with the space that we create between us
Love	Use compassion to heal any rifts in your relationship—this is the time to listen very carefully to your partner
Business	Fortify communication channels in the business—problems may have emerged from a lack of communication between departments
Lifestyle	Face your fears and become more flexible in your views

Hexagram 7
Shih (The Army)

The trigrams Earth over Water form the Shih hexagram. Water under the ground may either nourish or destabilize the surface. The I Ching equates this water source with a military force within a society. A nation with no means of protecting itself is clearly vulnerable. However, if its armed forces are poorly disciplined, trained or led, the nation will be weakened from within.

This hexagram stresses the need for conflict resolution before hostilities erupt, but Shih also recognizes that human failings frequently subvert any resolution. Since the most dedicated and effective troops may be led to defeat by weak, arrogant or reckless generals, Shih emphasizes the need for integrity in those placed in command. Similarly, those commanding the generals must be free of greed, impulsiveness and corruption. The honor of an army is largely reliant upon its national leaders' decisions. To prevail in an unjust war is no kind of victory at all. A society must therefore make very high demands upon the character of those in office.

The interdependence of the army and its commanders is reflected in all aspects of life where the many are led by the few. When we find ourselves in a position of leadership, it is necessary to be assured of the loyalty and trust of those who rely upon our guidance. We must earn and maintain this through our obvious concern and respect for our "forces" and our dedication to mutual benefit rather than personal gain.

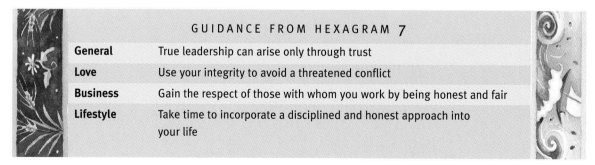

GUIDANCE FROM HEXAGRAM 7

General	True leadership can arise only through trust
Love	Use your integrity to avoid a threatened conflict
Business	Gain the respect of those with whom you work by being honest and fair
Lifestyle	Take time to incorporate a disciplined and honest approach into your life

Hexagram 8
Pi (Union)

Pi consists of Water over Earth. As the waters of the world move constantly across the planet to blend in rivers, lakes and oceans, so this hexagram represents the way in which individuals unite to form communities.

A droplet of water has little power, a rushing stream a moderate amount, and the crashing waves of the sea immense force. Likewise, a team or family may achieve more than the sum of its parts, and a harmonious nation very much more again. Pi asks us to examine how we contribute to our own community.

A successful community can be established with a shared sense of purpose, which will give it direction. The integration of the various individuals of the community is required for its stability. The bonds of trust and mutual assistance are imperative to unite it.

Self-interest is the primary obstacle to the formation of powerful communities, and more commonly arises from feelings of mistrust than from sheer greed. Therefore, to create effective unions, each individual needs to cultivate relationships built on respect, goodwill and generosity. This will benefit the self-esteem of friends, family and neighbors, and establish the sort of environment in which communal unity can flourish. The community should function as an extended family, with all members valued and supported, regardless of their specific roles.

GUIDANCE FROM HEXAGRAM 8

General	There is no more powerful force for positive change than a community bound by goodwill
Love	Focus on achieving unity in your relationship using goodwill and trust
Business	Look at strengthening industry networks
Lifestyle	Form or strengthen a small community of supportive friends and family

Hexagram 9
Hsiao Ch'u (The Taming Power of the Small)

Hsiao Ch'u comprises the trigrams Wind over Heaven. The image associated with this hexagram is of the insubstantial wind gently moving clouds through the sky. The changes in a cloudy sky are fleeting, and so Hsiao Ch'u informs us that, however we may try, this is not a time when we can expect to achieve great things. Enduring transformation will be possible only once we have developed our skills and power.

Life frequently presents us with conditions that impede the progress of our enterprises. When this occurs it is important not to be easily discouraged. More often than not these obstacles may be overcome by the persistent development of our knowledge, experience or strength. The obstacles will slow us down—but this is very different from their defeating us. The appropriate course of action in the face of such obstructions is to rest, prepare and learn. If progress cannot be achieved in the external world, it is best to attempt to make headway in our inner lives.

If this external inaction causes those around us to doubt our ability to realize our ambitions, it may be beneficial to persuade them gently to see the wisdom of this consolidation of our positions. The attitudes of others may prove to be among those small matters we should now be seeking to amend. Similarly, we must examine our dispositions, ensuring that we are not allowing our ambitions to undermine our patience and perseverance. Great lasting change is possible only through continuous attention to detail.

GUIDANCE FROM HEXAGRAM 9

General	When great change is impossible, energy is best directed to perfecting smaller matters
Love	Have fun with your relationships, developing your communication skills
Business	Assess whether there are areas in your business that require further attention or study
Lifestyle	Focus on developing your skills and strengths

Hexagram 10
Lu (Correct Conduct)

Lu is formed by the trigrams Heaven over Lake. Both of these symbols are in their appropriate positions, and are separated by sufficient distance to prevent any immediate clash of their natures. However, the inequality of the two trigrams may in time prove to cause disharmony, much as resentment grows in the underprivileged when they perceive their distance from the condition of the powerful and affluent.

Inequality and attendant jealousy appear in many areas of life other than wealth—the old may envy youth, the ill health, and the obscure fame. Society is fraught with imbalances that can give rise to enmity. Accordingly, Lu advises that we take the time to determine where our advantages lie and how we may best progress through life without treading on each other's toes. In fact, Lu goes so far as to suggest that a truly wise individual could walk on the tail of a tiger without causing it to bite.

Lu asks us to consider developing our social graces, warning us to tread our cautious way through a social minefield. This hexagram's advice is always to be mindful of our conduct, cultivating diplomacy, modesty and good humor. Our courteous behavior will mollify even the most difficult individual.

These social graces should be neither insincere nor a matter of mere form. When we treat each other considerately and with genuine respect, we will prevent countless potential difficulties and will step lightly and safely through life.

GUIDANCE FROM HEXAGRAM 10

General	If you take every step with care, a successful journey is ensured
Love	Goodwill is the key to lightening any relationship woes
Business	Courtesy and respect will help you achieve business success
Lifestyle	Work on alleviating any feelings of envy or jealousy

T'ai (Peace)

T'ai comprises the trigrams Earth over Heaven. One of the most auspicious hexagrams, it suggests that the harmonizing power of Heaven underlies all that is currently occurring in our everyday lives.

This indicates a time of personal and social tranquillity, during which imbalances and negative influences may be corrected almost effortlessly by the prevailing sense of goodwill. Pettiness, greed and anger will not thrive in this atmosphere of collective benevolence.

The Heavenly influence referred to in the I Ching can be interpreted as the inspiration we receive when we imagine our tumultuous world as healed and rebalanced. The essence of the I Ching, however, is the impermanence of all worldly situations, and so we are assured that the success boded by T'ai will, like a perfect day in Spring, have to end. Unlike the seasons, however, the conditions of our communal lives are largely within our power to shape and restore. When we are able to conjure up in the material world even a faint shadow of the imagined perfection of Heaven on Earth, this should be cause for celebration. It should also be a cause for quiet study of the circumstances that allowed the favorable state to occur.

Social harmony often results from the goodwill of various individuals, and T'ai emphasizes that each of us can strengthen this harmony by extending kindness and respect to those around us. Compassion, like aggression, is often contagious.

GUIDANCE FROM HEXAGRAM 11

General	Celebrate times of harmony, but do not neglect to study their causes
Love	Imbue your relationship with respect and kindness
Business	Analyze your business success and note how you achieved it
Lifestyle	This is a good time to do a kind deed for others

Hexagram 12
P'i (Stagnation)

P'i is formed by the trigrams Heaven over Earth. This is the reverse of hexagram 11, where Heaven's influence permeates the world. Hexagram 12 indicates the opposite of harmony. Here the qualities of Heaven lie high above our grasp, resulting in adversity, negativity and discouragement.

The hexagram's image of substance above and fragility beneath suggests unworthy people who come into positions of power during adversity, their outward shows of strength masking serious inner flaws. The weaker the sense of duty and honor in such individuals, the more likely they are to become arrogant, tyrannical and belligerent.

Like a building constructed on unstable foundations, these people will eventually be brought low by their own inadequacy. While they are able to maintain their worldly power, they may scorn, fear or persecute those of stronger character and greater integrity.

Another frequent strategy of corrupt leaders is to attempt to subvert the honor of more ethical individuals. P'i urges us to withstand all such coercions or temptations. Even if such collaboration were morally defensible, the benefits of aligning ourselves with so fallible a force would be very short-lived, and the damaging consequences far-reaching. From a practical as well as an ethical viewpoint, we would be far wiser to guard our consciences, await the inevitable improvement in conditions, and plan how to reverse whatever damage has been done.

GUIDANCE FROM HEXAGRAM 12

General	As all things bear the seeds of their opposites, there is hope even in the depths of adversity
Love	Be careful of falling in love with a person who is not what he or she seems
Business	Analyze any new business ventures—they may be too good to be true
Lifestyle	Strengthen your ethical and moral senses

Hexagram 13
T'ung Jen (Fellowship)

T'ung Jen comprises the trigrams Heaven over Fire. This suggests that we should try to stabilize our tumultuous feelings and passions into a more methodical expression of thoughts, inspired by the orderly movement of the sun and the constellations.

This hexagram combines aspects of hexagram 7, which relates to the leadership necessary to unite an army against a threat, and hexagram 8, which focuses on the inherent value of community. T'ung Jen's concern is how a community can be united and led in peacetime to achieve goals of value just as an army can be organized to defend its nation. Many challenges that would defeat individuals can be overcome through fellowship.

This hexagram often appears when we are called upon to organize numerous, perhaps wayward, individuals into a unified group. All can see the wisdom of co-operation, but are sometimes impeded by a lack of mutual trust. Suspicion and the concealment of our thoughts undermine the community spirit, and so T'ung Jen speaks of "fellowship in the open"; that is, in a place reflecting the opening of our hearts and minds to each other. As this occurs, various individuals will inevitably reveal fears, reservations and differences of opinion. If we are to be united, we need to reiterate the higher purpose we have in common, and respectfully ask that minor differences be put aside. Once a communal triumph has been achieved, many of these smaller disagreements will be forgotten.

GUIDANCE FROM HEXAGRAM 13

General	Dispel mistrust—this can mean achieving strength in numbers
Love	Work together to achieve a desired objective
Business	Communicate with your staff to dispel fears and misunderstandings
Lifestyle	Organize gatherings and workshops to develop communal spirit for a treasured project

Hexagram 14
Ta Yu (Abundance)

Ta Yu consists of the trigrams Fire over Heaven. This combination suggests the dazzling fires of the Sun illuminating the sky and the lands below, encouraging mental clarity, well-being and the growth of a healthy harvest.

Beneath the Sun's radiance, the obstacles to progress and prosperity have melted away, making this an opportune time for advancement with business and financial dealings. We will be able to discern solutions to previously worrying problems and to plan strategies to consolidate our gains. Our insight, intuition and sense of timing will all be functioning exceptionally well, and opportunities will present themselves as if of their own accord.

Some potential dangers still exist at this auspicious time. First among these is pride—when success is easily won, the ego may be over-inflated. Ta Yu warns us to beware of arrogance and greed when we enjoy abundance. Such behavior will alienate those who supported us in harder times, attract sycophants, and undermine the continuation of our success.

Another peril arises from taking our success too lightly and assuming that the current beneficial conditions will remain unchanged indefinitely. When this error takes hold, we may easily fritter away our newly won resources on unneeded or unhealthy luxuries.

Lasting abundance is best attained through preserving the harmonious conditions that originally gave rise to it. Generosity and humility are essential qualities in the genuinely successful.

GUIDANCE FROM HEXAGRAM 14

General	Those who understand the responsibilities of wealth are best able to maintain it
Love	Enjoy a harmonious period in your relationship, but do not become complacent
Business	Watch for golden opportunities to achieve business success, but do not be greedy
Lifestyle	Enjoy mental clarity, but also eliminate any feelings of arrogance and pride

Hexagram 15
Ch'ien (Humility)

Ch'ien comprises the trigrams Earth over Mountain. In the normal scheme of things, mountains tower over the surrounding countryside. In this hexagram, the natural order is reversed, suggesting that greatness may often be found in the most unobtrusive places and the most modest individuals. If we wish to establish a farm, for example, a superior location will be a quiet, fertile plain far beneath the majesty of a mountain range.

The majesty of the mountain is obvious, but the plain may hide greater treasures in its depths than do the peaks in their grandeur. Ch'ien advises us not to be misled by appearances, and elaborates on hexagram 14's praise for humility.

Pride in achievement is natural to the young, and in moderation is quite proper since it will fuel the desire to learn and to master new skills. In adults, however, the boastfulness of the child becomes more difficult to indulge. Self-importance and vanity may alienate others, to the point of blinding them to our real accomplishments. Humility, like self-discipline, is a quality we need to learn and nurture. This does not mean we ought to cultivate extremes of self-effacement—this may be a form of attention seeking in itself—but simply that we must be on our guard against ostentation and arrogance.

Our lives are not really comparable. The most skilled in one field may be hopelessly disadvantaged in many others. We should therefore acknowledge our achievements without feeling that they elevate us above the rest of our community.

GUIDANCE FROM HEXAGRAM 15

General	Arrogance is the enemy of true greatness
Love	Draw your loved one out of his or her shell
Business	Do not overlook the quiet achiever on your staff or the humble account in your portfolio
Lifestyle	Learn to look beneath the surface of things

Hexagram 16
Yu (Enthusiasm)

Yu comprises the trigrams Thunder over Earth. In the I Ching Thunder does not have negative associations; it symbolizes an outpouring of natural, invigorating energy. This hexagram therefore suggests the way a thunderstorm in Spring or early Summer often heralds the end of inactivity and the start of a new phase of growth. Before a rainstorm, tensions often run high, only to be released when the storm breaks.

By association, Yu also reflects the way in which energy within our community and ourselves can be raised and released by celebration or by the influence of a powerful motivator. Like approaching thunder, this exuberance changes our environment, enlivening it and increasing our confidence in our power to take action.

Secular and religious ceremonies and festivities are commonly used to generate this type of energy. Most cultures have developed a complex system of observances and rituals for various occasions. These help to unite the community in shared activities, at the same time reaffirming the distinctive nature of the cultures of different individuals. From the Pope at Easter to a parent arranging a birthday party, those who officiate at or arrange such festive landmarks in the year are typically held in esteem for their contributions. Strong leadership never underestimates the power of shared enthusiasm.

When our spirits are buoyed up by these outpourings of energy, our community will have increased confidence in its power to overcome future difficulties.

GUIDANCE FROM HEXAGRAM 16	
General	Celebration will revitalize the spirit
Love	Suggest a surprise outing to your partner
Business	Make a point of acknowledging and celebrating the achievements of your business
Lifestyle	Throw a party or have a seasonal celebration to honor the cycle of nature

Hexagram 17
Sui (Following)

Sui is formed by the Lake trigram over the Thunder trigram. The natural position of these two forces has been reversed. This suggests that thunder with its invigorating power (see hexagram 16) has willingly humbled itself in order to achieve a subtler effect. Its influence in Sui is symbolized by the movement of gently rippling waves on the surface of a lake, which are the only indication of the quiet, persistent power acting from beneath.

In the same way, a judicious leader will exert influence with delicacy when necessary. He or she will lead by example rather than by issuing orders, and will think in terms of gradual rather than sudden progress, ensuring that activity and rest are well balanced. Recuperation from labor is necessary to us all, however impatient we may feel to press ahead. This impatience is preferable to the dampening of enthusiasm occasioned by exhaustion.

Effective leaders are not deluded about their role. They lead to serve, rather than to appease their own egos or indulge a desire for power. Rulers should see themselves in a position less exalted than that of the humblest servant, since their obligations extend to every individual in their community rather than to a single employer.

To lead well, we must learn the needs of those who wish to follow. We may feel that their desires need correcting at times. If we do, we must persuade gently rather than riding roughshod over those who trust us. Coercion and force can only breed opposition.

GUIDANCE FROM HEXAGRAM 17

General	When leadership flows equally from the heart and mind, steady progress will be assured
Love	Be gentle with your partner and show what you need by example rather than with harsh words
Business	Balance hard labor with rest and recuperation
Lifestyle	Map out a plan of action that incorporates rest and gradual progress

Hexagram 18
Ku (Restoring that which has Degenerated)

Ku comprises the Mountain trigram over the Wind trigram. It suggests a low wind traveling across the land, its passage impeded by an imposing mountain. As if in frustration, the wind will cause damage to the vegetation at the foot of the mountain.

In personal and social terms, Ku relates to situations that arise when our progress is hindered. We encounter obstacles that have been allowed to grow unchecked through neglect and indolence. Stagnation and decay will prevail unless we are prepared to root out the causes of the damage and make reparations. Since the specific types of problems Ku describes have resulted from failures or injuries in the past, this hexagram urges us to examine both our community and our own natures for such unresolved issues. This analysis may be accompanied by feelings of guilt or resentment. Such emotions should not be indulged, since they waste energy better directed to correcting the poor habits, prejudices or phobias that cause problems. While these mountainous obstructions need prompt attention if the degeneration is to be reversed, we need to take time to identify their true sources correctly. Healing is dependent upon accurate diagnosis. If the cause is misidentified or dealt with cursorily, the destructive cycle will continue—to the detriment of all. Thoroughness, rather than short-term solutions, is called for.

Although Ku refers to very trying and chaotic circumstances, it reassures us that this is a great opportunity for restoration, recovery and reconciliation.

GUIDANCE FROM HEXAGRAM 18

General	To approach the future with confidence, address the problems of the past
Love	This is an excellent time to reconcile your differences with your partner
Business	If your business is feeling stagnant, take the time to identify the true source of the damage
Lifestyle	Take some time to work on releasing a bad habit, an assumption or a phobia that is holding you back

Hexagram 19
Lin (Approach)

Lin is formed by the placement of Earth over Lake. This suggests the image of a lake being cradled protectively in high ground. The peaceful coexistence of these two powers suggests the meeting of two inexhaustible sources of wisdom, embodied by the depth of the waters and the bounty of the Earth.

The situation described by Lin is one in which we are favored by both circumstances and individuals of greater experience and power than ourselves. We can benefit greatly from seizing this opportunity to learn from both types of influences. The conditions are like those of early Spring, when expansion and prosperity seem almost inevitable and success appears certain.

Such auspicious circumstances cannot last indefinitely, so the hexagram urges to take the fullest possible advantage of them while we can. Lin warns of a future reversal of fortune as inevitable as the coming of another Winter. It also recommends that we look in the present for the seeds of future problems so that we are well equipped to deal with them when they arise. With sufficient foresight many difficulties can be prevented from growing to unmanageable proportions. For these reasons, we must not allow ourselves to fritter away the potentiality of Spring by simply dozing in the sunshine. Favorable conditions should be enjoyed, but not at the expense of inattention toward our mentors. We must also ensure that the gains we achieve are shared with our families, friends and communities. The kindness of this season must be reflected in our own natures.

GUIDANCE FROM HEXAGRAM 19

General	Steady advancement is a matter of learning to recognize favorable opportunities
Love	This is the time to deepen your insights into your relationship
Business	Business expansion and success are possible at this time
Lifestyle	Take the time to listen to those with experience and wisdom

Hexagram 20
Kuan (Observation)

Kuan is formed by the trigrams Wind over Earth. The I Ching associates the freedom of the wind, as it crosses the surface of the land, with the thoughts and perception of an individual who watches for the changes in the environment and reflects on their effects.

This theme of watchfulness is reflected in Kuan's shape, which resembles that of a traditional Chinese tower. Such a tower afforded an impressive view over the countryside, and was also, for the population surrounding them, a prominent feature of the landscape. In the same way, this hexagram suggests both the expanded perception of the ruler and his example to the rest of the community. In our own ways we all benefit from the tranquil contemplation of our environment.

There is the danger, however, that we will become overly detached from the world when we view it from an elevated perspective. The watcher may become alienated from the community if he or she remains in isolation in the tower. A withdrawn spirit will eventually sicken for the nourishment of everyday existence, and its perception will become distorted through distance. Dangers may then grow unnoticed.

For this reason, Kuan reminds us to alternate our meditative isolation with travel throughout our environment, like the untethered wind. An accurate assessment of circumstances can be made only when we study our world both at close range and from afar. An unchanging perspective can provide a partial picture only.

GUIDANCE FROM HEXAGRAM 20

General	To understand your role in the world, remain alert to all that affects you
Love	Rebalance your feelings of isolation by making the effort to go out among your community
Business	Take the time to go out into the community or your customer base to refamiliarize yourself with what your clients need
Lifestyle	Balance times of isolation with travel

Hexagram 21
Shih Ho (Biting Through)

Shih Ho comprises the trigrams Fire over Thunder. This suggests bursts of lightning amid a thunderstorm. As in hexagram 16, the thunderstorm is viewed as a force that liberates energy. Here, also, the storm is likened to the power needed to correct social imbalances, the lightning representing the flashes of insight required for clarifying complex issues and the thunder suggesting the force needed to uphold judgment.

The shape of Shih Ho plays a part in its interpretation in the I Ching. Hexagram 27, comprising yang lines at the top and bottom and four yin lines in between, is likened to an open mouth. Shih Ho is like an opened mouth whose lips or teeth cannot close because of an obstruction (the other yang line in the Fire trigram). For the upper and lower lips to meet, the obstacle must be bitten through.

Similarly, when injustice or crime forms a barrier to the harmonious linking of individuals within the community, it must be firmly eradicated. This process, however, must not be taken lightly, or it will itself lead to further disharmony. For this reason, a system of justice must be scrupulously impartial and honorable. Then it will function effectively.

The lightning further symbolizes the clarity with which a community's laws and penalties must be stated, and the thunder the energy needed to see that these are administered fairly and conscientiously. Shih Ho further reminds us that this model of justice must exist in all aspects of our culture, not merely in the law itself.

GUIDANCE FROM HEXAGRAM 21	
General	Harmony is unattainable without justice
Love	If you have been unjustly treated it is time to stand up for yourself
Business	Watch for fraud or other crime against your business
Lifestyle	Meditate so you will receive insight into ways of resolving complex issues

Hexagram 22
Pi (Grace)

Pi is formed by the placement of the trigrams Mountain over Fire. In this image, the mountain is lit dramatically by the rising or setting sun or by a blazing fire on its foothills, and its grandeur is enhanced. This hexagram therefore relates to the appreciation and accentuation of beauty.

Many of our aesthetic preferences are based on an appreciation for the harmony of proportions and textures. Accordingly, the I Ching praises the contemplation of beauty as a means of leading us away from the disturbing and chaotic aspects of life. Observing natural grace will inspire us to emulate it in our lives and actions.

Pi warns us, however, about the danger of overemphasizing surface resplendence at the expense of the more enduring internal qualities. To be dazzled by superficial beauty will lead in time to superficial thought and behavior. This may in turn give rise to errors of judgment, with our values determined by false criteria and our treatment of others characterized by prejudice. External beauty pleases because it reflects, albeit faintly, the condition of spiritual grace. It is therefore ironic that exaggerating its importance can so easily lead us in the opposite direction. Beauty is a powerful force of attraction, and so Pi advises us not to see it as an end in itself. There is little point in relying on beauty's allure; the most abiding beauty is seen more often with the heart than with the eye.

GUIDANCE FROM HEXAGRAM 22

General	By valuing beauty you will cultivate your taste for harmony in all facets of life
Love	Do not be taken in by superficial appearances—look deeply into other people's character
Business	Do not be tempted by a dazzling proposal—check to see if it is as strong as it looks
Lifestyle	Cultivate your internal beauty

Hexagram 23
Po (Splitting Apart)

Po consists of the trigrams Mountain over Earth. The image associated with this hexagram is that of a steep, narrow mountain standing alone over a plain, exposed to the force of the elements that will eventually bring it down through steady erosion.

This hexagram cautions that, as the endurance of even a mountain is finite, human accomplishments are far more fleeting. However strongly we build, all our structures will disintegrate in time. This is reflected in the shape of the hexagram, which the I Ching likens to that of a house, the walls of which have split apart. The structure has been undermined and is now held together solely by the yang line representing the roof.

A building, or a situation, that has fallen upon such hard times is no longer worth attempting to save. Bereft of internal support, its final collapse is only a matter of time. To abandon a project in which we had our hopes and energy invested is always painful, but Po emphasizes that we should try not to be incapacitated by our distress. Though the current situation is doomed, we should waste no time in formulating new strategies, integrating the lessons we have learnt from this setback.

Human beings have enormous innate resilience and adaptation. The very act of walking is a matter of falling forward and then recovering our balance. Disaster will lie not in the falling implied by this hexagram, but solely in our failure to regain our balance afterward.

GUIDANCE FROM HEXAGRAM 23

General	New enterprises must often wait for the collapse of the old
Love	Your current relationship, or a particular issue within the relationship, should be abandoned
Business	Your current course has become troublesome and needs to be revised
Lifestyle	Consider backing away from a troublesome situation—learn a positive lesson from having to walk away

Hexagram 24
Fu (The Turning Point)

Fu comprises the trigrams Earth over Thunder. The revitalizing energy of thunder is felt within the earth, awakening it from a long period of dormancy. This imagery caused the composers of the I Ching to associate Fu with the Winter Solstice, the shortest day of the year. Once the Solstice has been passed, the daylight hours gradually begin to lengthen, despite the deepening of Winter. We are given the assurance that light will be restored to the world.

The previous hexagram connotes the depth of darkness. Fu represents the gradual improvement that must necessarily follow. This progress will unfold without our effort. Like the lengthening of days after the Winter Solstice, its effects will be felt only gradually. It will, however, be similarly unstoppable.

It is futile to hurry progress. We should instead use this period of quiet to cultivate patience and develop strategies for the Spring. The time of the Winter Solstice is traditionally a time of resting and celebration of renewal, just as it is in Northern Hemisphere Christianity, where the shortest day heralds the festivities of Christmas and New Year. This hexagram reminds us of the wisdom of treating new beginnings with care. Just as a person recovering from illness and injury must not fall into the error of overexertion, so we should consider this time in terms of slow but continual advancement.

All movement is seen by the I Ching as cyclic, and Fu is the hexagram of returning to the beginning with all the enthusiasm of one reborn.

GUIDANCE FROM HEXAGRAM 24

General	When steady improvement is unfolding naturally, you should not feel the need to push matters
Love	New romance will be rekindled in your life
Business	Business will slowly improve over the next few months
Lifestyle	Take time to make plans for the future

Hexagram 25

Wu Wang (Innocence)

Wu Wang is formed by Heaven over Thunder. The regenerative power of thunder as it rejuvenates the earth in Spring suggests a heavenly blessing being bestowed.

This hexagram indicates innocent pleasure in our own strength. A child or young animal will run for pleasure rather than to achieve a purpose, win a race or impress others. This joy in motion and absolute focus on the present has the power to correct the imbalances set up by our habits of overly complex analysis and scheming.

When we act solely to gain advantage or the approval of others, we will undermine our efforts. Too much of the mind is focusing on an imagined future, hoping for reward or dreading failure. However, if we focus on and honor the effort of each aspect of our work, we will remain open to inspiration and alert to error, instead of having our thoughts scattered by doubts and expectations.

Wu Wang acknowledges the value of forethought and planning, but reminds us that we can never allow for every contingency. A growing plant maneuvers around obstacles, rather than balking at them until it can devise a strategy. Adjusting to conditions from moment to moment is preferable to filling our minds with contingency plans that may never be needed. This requires us to cultivate trust in ourselves and the guiding force behind life. Wu Wang encourages us to find a balance between this childlike confidence and the wisdom of experience.

GUIDANCE FROM HEXAGRAM 25

General	You will function most effectively when fully present in each moment
Love	Have fun just for the sake of it
Business	Let go of overly complex schemes—sometimes the simple approach is best
Lifestyle	Enjoy what you do in your life

Hexagram 26
Ta Ch'u (The Taming Power of the Great)

Ta Ch'u comprises the trigrams Mountain over Heaven. The image of the bounty of Heaven being contained beneath or within a mountain suggests a cavern full of hidden treasure. This accumulated wealth is the result of the self-discipline, prudence and forethought of those in the past, so Ta Ch'u advises us to seek wisdom and guidance from those who have gone before us in order to provide for the future.

When the development of personal wealth, virtue and knowledge are a matter of daily routine, we build up not only our resources but also the self-discipline necessary for achieving our goals. In contrast, if we spend impulsively and frivolously and neglect to nourish our minds and spirits, this will lessen our chances of accomplishing anything of enduring value.

While this hexagram recommends the accrual of resources, it does not advocate avarice or hoarding. Wealth, like wisdom, should be put to work and shared wisely. Ta Ch'u is a hexagram of restraint and judiciousness rather than stagnation. It advises moderation so that we can assure the care and sustenance of our family, friends and community.

Achieving a correct balance in these matters requires firmness, decisiveness and strong leadership. When these qualities are utilized for the common good, we will embody many of the characteristics of the virtuous ruler, sadly so often lacking in those who achieve positions of power. Ta Ch'u is in many respects the hexagram of that rare and highly valued creature, the altruistic politician.

GUIDANCE FROM HEXAGRAM 26

General	The disciplined accumulation of wisdom and resources will strengthen you in all future endeavors
Love	Being impulsive or frivolous will not serve you in your relationship
Business	Use self-discipline in your decision making and seek guidance from those who have experience within your profession
Lifestyle	Focus on building up your inner resources and strengths

Hexagram 27

I (Nourishment)

I is formed by the arrangement of Mountain over Thunder. The thunder felt at the base of the mountain represents energy, which rises from below to ascend to great heights. This hexagram reflects the invigorating nutrients within the earth that encourage the flourishing of vegetation. Much of this vegetation will in turn be used to sustain, protect and heal us all.

The shape of the hexagram, which suggests an open mouth, emphasizes the concept of nutrition. The yang lines at the top and bottom represent parted lips or teeth, and the four enclosed yin lines a mouth either ready to receive food or opening to speak.

Since our words and ideas may be a source of sustenance and encouragement to each other, I sees them as the counterpart of the nourishment we take through our food. In both speech and diet, the hexagram stresses the need for discrimination, moderation and high quality of contents. Just as ill-chosen or excessive meals trouble the digestion, so does thoughtless, immoderate speech disquiet the mind. Similarly, we may find our emotions and spirits suffering when we feed them a diet of delusion, intolerance, vanity and superficiality. There is "junk food" of the mind and soul as well as the body, and it is equally destructive.

We are our most powerful when both spirit and body are well-tended. In thought and nutrition, our goal should be the tranquil, effective digestion of worthy ingredients.

GUIDANCE FROM HEXAGRAM 27	
General	Discrimination is as necessary in the spiritual diet as it is in the physical
Love	Be careful that your thoughts and words in your relationship are well chosen and tolerant
Business	By using the right words you will gain encouragement and sustenance
Lifestyle	Consider removing from your life all that is not worthy

Hexagram 28
Ta Kuo (The Preponderance of the Great)

Ta Kuo is formed by the placement of the trigrams Lake over Wind. This reversal of the natural order suggests extraordinary but temporary circumstances, such as the rising of the lake's waters during a flood to the upper reaches of the surrounding trees ó the usual realm of the breeze.

The danger implicit in this image is also expressed in the shape of the hexagram. The creators of the I Ching likened Ta Kuo to an old and overly stressed wooden beam. The four yang lines indicate strength in the middle, but the yin lines at the top and bottom warn of weakness at both ends. If such timber is the main support for a house's roof, the situation must be addressed rapidly—or disaster will follow.

Unfortunately, Ta Kuo suggests that the time for repair to a situation has passed and our only course is to vacate the area, just as we would flee from a collapsing building or retreat from rising floodwaters. The hexagram will frequently indicate a situation in which we have allowed ambition to overtax our resources and capabilities. Cutting our losses and withdrawing from the enterprise is the wisest move, however distressing or distasteful this might seem.

If we act pragmatically and decisively, misfortune may eventually prove only to have been a setback. We put ourselves at great risk, however, if we postpone our retreat or remain obstinately in the present situation. Self-sacrifice at this point would achieve nothing.

GUIDANCE FROM HEXAGRAM 28

General	Alertness and timely intervention will forestall many misfortunes
Love	A conflict that has not been resolved may require you to leave the situation temporarily
Business	You will need to retreat from a troublesome project or business situation
Lifestyle	Let go of the present situation and assess your ambitions

Hexagram 29

K'an (The Abyss)

K'an consists of the trigrams Water over Water. Where water exists in such abundant quantity, it will often conceal dangers in its darkened depths. Its downward force will open and expand the crevices it fills, creating hazardous caverns and trenches. Darkness, cold and crushing pressure are all conditions we find in the depths, and consequently the predominant message of K'an is inauspicious.

At the same time, this hexagram counsels us that observing the nature of water may guide us in our formulation of strategies even in the midst of peril and doubt. Until water has reached the lowest position it can occupy, it is in constant motion, washing away or flowing around obstacles in its quest for its destination. Even in stagnant pools, water continues its purpose, gradually seeping down, permeating its boundaries or changing its nature to escape its confinement as vapor and begin its journey once again as rain.

If we can emulate the persistence, dependability and adaptability of water, our trials may strengthen us. If we can resist panic and despair, encounters with threats will sharpen our awareness, encourage ingenuity and resourcefulness, and prepare us for further trials that await us. At this difficult time K'an urges us to acclimatize ourselves to danger, like those who work in hazardous professions, cultivating calmness, a positive outlook and strong survival skills. It is important to do this rather than surrendering to dismay or inertia.

GUIDANCE FROM HEXAGRAM 29	
General	When you can learn from danger, you will triumph over it
Love	Avoid emotional outbursts—do not overreact or allow arguments to spiral into violence or depression
Business	This is a dangerous time for your business—stay calm, as there is always a way of resolving issues
Lifestyle	Use meditation and calming techniques to help you find creative solutions to your current problems

Hexagram 30
Li (Brilliance)

Li consists of the trigrams Fire over Fire. While hexagram 29, formed from two Water trigrams, suggests downward motion and danger, Li suggests the uplifting energy of flames and the surmounting of our difficulties. Just as light pours over the objects in its path, creativity and insight illuminate the darker aspects of our lives and help us to negotiate our paths.

All fires, from the humblest campfire to the stars themselves, rely on a steady supply of appropriate fuel. The fire of our enthusiasm is no exception to this rule. We must therefore learn how best to feed the flames so that they neither falter into smoldering cinders nor run dangerously wild.

Just as our distant ancestors acquired mastery of fire through careful observation rather than a deep understanding of physics and chemistry, so we can learn how to control our own inner fires through patient attention. Gentle mindfulness of our previous successes and errors will help us find enlightenment.

Every fire, like every human life, is finite. However, just as a flame may be taken from one candle to light another, the enthusiasm and wisdom of individuals can pass from person to person, adding to our collective enlightenment. While searching for inner brightness, we must avoid the error of self-obsession. Like a cheering communal bonfire, the light and warmth of the spirit should be shared.

GUIDANCE FROM HEXAGRAM 30

General	By tending the fires of the mind and spirit you will illuminate your path
Love	Enjoy this time of inspiration and delight, feeling enthusiasm for your partner's development
Business	This is a time when creative solutions to business issues will come to fruition if you are fueled with enthusiasm
Lifestyle	Join in communal activities that help enhance your creativity

Hexagram 31

Hsien (Courtship)

Hsien is formed by the trigrams Lake over Mountain. The image of a mountaintop lake suggests that the strong yang energy of the peak has been balanced and made more receptive by the calming yin energy of the lake. This suggests strength joined with openness and humility, and is a very favorable combination. The image also suggests the raising of the gentle by the powerful, just as the lake is elevated above its natural position and presented to the heavens.

All men and women comprise a blend of yin and yang qualities, but Hsien simplifies matters, equating the yin of the Lake to women, the yang of the Mountain to men, and the hexagram as a whole to the harmonious relationship of a courting couple. When a couple is well matched, each, like the lake on the mountain, balances the other's nature.

When attraction arises between individuals they are usually responding to the perception that their respective qualities are both shared and complementary. If only one of these aspects is present, the relationship will soon be undermined by a lack of stimulation or by excessive dependency. A pairing is also unlikely to last if its basis is predominantly physical.

While Hsien often alludes to actual romance and marriages, it also emphasizes our need to seek tempering influences and to imbue all our interactions with some of the mutual honor, respect and affection that bind couples together. Selfless love is a power never to be underestimated.

GUIDANCE FROM HEXAGRAM 31

General	When attraction is strengthened by mutual respect and support, success is assured
Love	You are well matched if your love has a blend of shared and complementary qualities
Business	You may wish to seek a partnership that complements your strengths
Lifestyle	Seek to cultivate respect and honor toward and within those around you

Hexagram 32
Heng (Constancy)

Heng comprises the trigrams Thunder over Wind. Neither storms nor winds have any permanency, but both are certain to reappear. Thunder is thought of in the I Ching as a powerful, invigorating force, while Wind is considered to embody gentleness. Through this alternation of presence and absence, power and temperance, Heng suggests that only change endures.

Our bodies function through a succession of cycles—inhalation and exhalation, tension and relaxation, expansion and contraction—and the world is governed by the cycles of nature. In our enterprises, we often forget that we should be prepared for change, and fall into the error of equating stubbornness with persistence. If a strategy fails we often repeat it, in the mistaken belief that this demonstrates strength of character rather than obduracy. Heng reminds us that true endurance requires constant activity, thought and reinvention, rather than mental stagnancy.

The goal of true endurance is not the removal of obstacles. The difficulties we encounter maintain our adaptability, requiring us to participate in constant self-renewal rather than surrendering to inertia. Enduring works in all fields of human achievement result from countless obstacles overcome successfully. Effortless work is soon forgotten.

Heng also elaborates on hexagram 31, moving from the image of courtship to that of a long and successful marriage. This is another model of durability that is unworkable when ruled by inertia, but easily achievable through continual, harmonious change.

GUIDANCE FROM HEXAGRAM 32

General	True persistence is neither habit nor obstinacy, but a process of constant renewal
Love	Adapt to the changes around you to deepen your relationship
Business	Your effort in business matters will be rewarded
Lifestyle	Take the time to avoid inertia and work toward self-renewal

Hexagram 33
Tun (Retreat)

Tun is formed by the trigrams Heaven over Mountain. The mountain may be imagined as an earthly force challenging the majesty of Heaven. Rather than engaging in an undignified and pointless struggle, Heaven maintains its distance from the topmost peaks, which by their nature are unable to reach any higher.

The message of this hexagram is that the worthiest response is often withdrawal beyond the reach of an adversary. In the Oriental martial arts, it is well understood that the masters of the various forms will be those who most rarely engage in combat. Such people would see no honor in defeating someone they knew to be less skilled, or in putting those under their protection in danger by engaging them in an unequal battle. Less well-trained warriors, unable to distinguish cowardice from an objective and practical response to dire circumstances, will often allow pride to goad them into fights that are better avoided. Tun urges us not to fall into this error. The cowardly course of action is flight with no intention of re-engagement or, worse, compromise and collaboration with those we know to be tyrannical and unjust.

There is no disgrace—and much wisdom—in retreating temporarily, either to forestall an unnecessary and potentially destructive confrontation or to avoid a certain defeat. In the latter case, Tun emphasizes that we must resist provocation, anger and impulsiveness, and instead coolly withdraw to plan an effective counteroffensive.

GUIDANCE FROM HEXAGRAM 33

General	Retreating from an unequal struggle is not an admission of defeat
Love	If you feel that your partner has been unjust, take time to strengthen your position before engaging in a fight
Business	Do not compromise—instead, retreat to rethink your strategies before reentering negotiations
Lifestyle	Avoid a destructive confrontation, but take the time to construct an effective strategy for dealing with the issue—do not ignore it

Hexagram 34
Ta Chuang (The Power of the Great)

Ta Chuang comprises the trigrams Thunder over Heaven. Stormclouds ascending to the heights of the firmament suggest both upward movement and a gathering of strength. This imagery can also be seen in the structure of the hexagram.

Yang lines appear to be arising from the base of the hexagram, as if the yang lines of the lower trigram are beginning to influence the upper. The peace we see in hexagram 11—with the wholly yin trigram (Earth) above the wholly yang trigram (Heaven)—has given way to vigorous activity. Ta Chuang suggests a course of action quite the reverse of that of hexagram 33. It urges us to take advantage of favorable conditions and increasing strength in order to tackle opposition directly. However, since the prevailing energy has similarities to that of a brash, eager young man, the hexagram also counsels us to be wary of overconfidence, rashness and a narcissistic delight in our ability to wield force. This is especially the case when we are feeling empowered again after a period of inactivity.

Warriors should be judged not by how much damage they can inflict upon an opposing force, but by how little harm they need to do before achieving their purpose. Any fool can order a barrage of artillery to destroy an enemy encampment. It takes vastly more skill and wisdom to take control by capturing key positions, thereby minimizing misery and suffering. The former course is simpler, but dishonors the irresponsible victor.

GUIDANCE FROM HEXAGRAM 34	
General	Advantages can be won when you accompany increasing strength with responsible action
Love	You will find yourself powerfully attractive to others—use this power wisely
Business	This is a favorable time for business, but do not overstep your advantages to the unwarranted detriment of those around you
Lifestyle	If you tackle any problematic issues with compassion and honor, you will be successful

Hexagram 35

Chin (Progress)

Chin is formed by the placement of Fire over Earth. The image suggested by this configuration is that of the sunrise. Just as the dawn arrives without effort but to enormous effect, so have we now entered into a period of steady, unforced advancement. The progress achieved at such a time can be as significant as the changing of night into day, and will take surprisingly little work to accomplish.

The danger here is that we may find this easy progress either unsatisfying or the cause for complacency. To avoid these pitfalls, Chin encourages us to maintain the same inner tranquillity in the face of victory as the I Ching urges in adversity.

The alternation of opposite conditions is in the nature of life, and we therefore require levelheadedness in both success and affliction. This will prevent us from surrendering the control of our inner lives to external occurrences. To triumph without a challenge will not diminish the progress made. As long as we acknowledge that we were aided by good fortune, and that this may fail to assist our next enterprise, we are unlikely to slip into either discontent or vanity.

Chin also emphasizes that we must not take advantage of these conditions of rapid and easy change for personal gain, but must keep our attention on the furtherance of shared objectives. As the rising sun provides light and warm for all, so we should ensure that we pass our successes on to our families, friends and community.

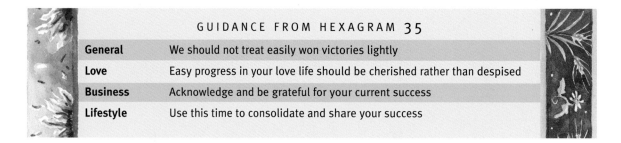

GUIDANCE FROM HEXAGRAM 35	
General	We should not treat easily won victories lightly
Love	Easy progress in your love life should be cherished rather than despised
Business	Acknowledge and be grateful for your current success
Lifestyle	Use this time to consolidate and share your success

Hexagram 36
Ming I (The Darkening of the Light)

Ming I is formed by the trigrams Earth over Fire. This hexagram represents the sun's setting, a reverse of hexagram 35, which represents the sun's rising. Similarly, the meaning of Ming I is a reversal of the previous hexagram—Chin's depiction of a time of effortless progress is replaced by a period of darkness and obstruction.

To travel by night is usually a more arduous undertaking than journeying in the sunlight. Ming I suggests that we cannot realistically expect to advance our projects at this time. If at all possible, we should postpone any further attempts until a more auspicious period. It is important to keep in mind that auspicious periods must eventually follow, just as daybreak will inevitably end the night.

The darkness of this time often reflects the darkness in the minds or spirits of people around us, particularly those in positions of authority or power. As such people are currently in ascendance, this is not the time to challenge them directly. We should by no means collaborate with them, but it would be wise to conceal our true natures, beliefs and intentions in order to avoid reprisals. When we travel through enemy territory by night, we would do well to conceal our light.

Accordingly, Ming I advocates an attitude of detachment rather than of confrontation or deception. Our wisest course is to attempt to buy ourselves time without compromising our integrity, protecting our endangered candle until the sun arises to herald a new dawn.

GUIDANCE FROM HEXAGRAM 36	
General	In the midst of danger we may need to conceal our light in order to avoid detection
Love	This is not a time to show your true feelings—detach yourself from the issue
Business	Do not start any new ventures during this time—you will only be obstructed
Lifestyle	Work on your inner strengths until the obstructions pass

Hexagram 37

Chia Jen (The Family)

Chia Jen comprises the trigrams Wind over Fire. This hexagram suggests the image of air rising from a blazing hearth to keep a house warm at night. The flames are the source of the heat, but require the circulating air to transfer the heat through the rooms. This is equated in the I Ching to the way in which our thoughts and emotions (Fire) are transmitted through speech (Wind).

Words, however, are powerful only when the attitudes that generate them are worthy. The circulating air will bring little comfort if the fire is not well tended and fueled. It is the individual's duty to see that these internal fires of the spirit are well maintained. Sincere and courteous communication is essential to all levels of society, from families to nations. Chia Jen stresses the importance of language for making clear to every member of a collective his or her individual roles and responsibilities.

The I Ching was written in an era when the roles of men and women and the mature were more rigid than they are in western culture today. It uses the traditional model of the family to illustrate this sense of appropriate duty. However, it is perfectly applicable to all types of effective teamwork if we look at its emphasis on the balance of yin and yang qualities, the responsibilities of the powerful toward the weaker and the deference of the less experienced to the more worldly.

GUIDANCE FROM HEXAGRAM 37	
General	Teamwork can flourish only under the influence of open and respectful communication
Love	Develop a form of sincere communication that will benefit your relationship
Business	Make sure that each member in your team understands his or her role in the project, so that misunderstandings do not occur
Lifestyle	Assess whether you are communicating clearly and effectively with those important to you

Hexagram 38
K'uei (Opposition)

K'uei consists of the trigrams Fire over Lake. Since flames rise and water descends, the two elements cannot commingle. Accordingly, K'uei warns of division and factionalism.

The lake will not drown the fire, nor will the fire evaporate the water—Fire and Lake cannot influence each other. Indifference and a willful refusal to communicate can bring all progress to a standstill.

Our current position may be either outside this dynamic or as a member of one of the opposing parties, but in either case K'uei advises that the only course is to work toward reconciliation. Since groups divided by gulfs of communication become increasingly inclined to demonize the opposition, the first duty is to try to instill an element of mutual respect so that individuals can agree to disagree. This is rarely the simplest of tasks, and K'uei makes it clear that small victories are the best we can hope for initially.

Extreme tactfulness is required, especially if we have aligned ourselves with one side or the other. We must be scrupulously unbiased, focusing on precluding emotional outbursts and reiterating the need for unity if progress is to recommence. Regardless of how others are behaving, the most disastrous error at this time is to allow ourselves to be provoked into anger or discourtesy. A moment's ill-considered outburst could greatly harm our credibility. Only when our behavior is exemplary and our motives clear can we hope to make headway.

GUIDANCE FROM HEXAGRAM 38	
General	When disunity reigns, reconciliation must become the priority
Love	Use extreme tact to overcome a potentially divisive issue
Business	Stagnation in business may be the result of a refusal to communicate effectively—remedy this before the business can progress again
Lifestyle	Check to see if you can start resolving the crisis in your life by learning to respect your "enemy"

Chien (Obstruction)

Chien is constructed by the placement of Water over Mountain. The nature of spring water on a mountaintop is to stream downward as quickly as it can. Chien, however, suggests a watercourse that cannot move quickly as obstacles block its course. It can only break free once rain or rivulets have increasd its volume sufficiently.

This imagery relates to periods in our lives when the barriers to our progress are insurmountable. This situation is likely to remain in force until, like the obstructed stream, we are either empowered by the aid of others or have gathered enough internal force to overpower the obstructions. Chien recommends that, although external assistance may eventually materialize, we should concentrate on gathering our strength, and take advantage of our immobility to spend some time on self-examination and introspection. When we do so, we are likely at first to encounter both self-pity and frustration. These should be kept firmly in check, as should the tendency to apportion blame. It is far wiser to examine our own natures, attempting to find and correct any flaws or errors that could have contributed to our circumstances. In this way, we will become stronger even as we are halted in our tracks.

Once our circumstances have altered to our advantage, we should begin to move forward cautiously. Danger may still lie ahead.

GUIDANCE FROM HEXAGRAM 39

General	When outward progress is impossible, the best course is to cultivate your internal strengths
Love	When love goes sour, look into yourself for clues on how to build a better relationship
Business	Do not blame others for any problems in business; instead, gather support and ideas on how to solve the issue
Lifestyle	Do not allow obstacles to make you feel sorry for yourself—this is a temporary setback only

Hexagram 40
Hsieh (Deliverance)

Hsieh comprises Thunder over Water. In the I Ching, bodies of water frequently represent places of danger, and thunder signifies a call to action. This hexagram therefore signifies movement away from hazardous conditions.

The image of the thunderstorm is also used to represent the releasing of tension. This, however, will only be a temporary reprieve at this time and advantage should be taken of this brief improvement of your situation.

This trigram suggests that recent difficulties have left us in a weakened condition, and a period of convalescence is needed before we resume our progress. Complacency would currently be destructive, as would any attempt to gain further ground. Our appropriate course is to seek a place of safety. The challenge to a recovering patient or a newly freed prisoner is to readapt to everyday life. Only when a sense of normality has been restored should such a person attempt more rigorous undertakings.

As we embark on this journey of rehabilitation, Hsieh advises us to free our hearts and minds of the burdens of the past. Harboring guilt or resentment will only slow our flight and delay our recovery. Whether our trials were caused by ourselves or by others, if we are to be genuinely free we need to be able to forgive unwise or unworthy acts and omissions. If these errors and misdeeds are not washed away by the cleansing storm, they will prove distracting at a time when our minds must remain clear. Our problems are receding, but we have not reached our sanctuary quite yet.

GUIDANCE FROM HEXAGRAM 40	
General	On a flight to freedom, you would do well to discard the millstones of grievance and recrimination
Love	Do not allow guilt or recriminations to get in the way of your relationship
Business	Take small steps when rebuilding a problematic business undertaking
Lifestyle	Take the time to release past issues and resentments

Hexagram 41

Sun (Decrease)

Sun is formed by the trigrams Mountain over Lake. As the waters of a lake at the foot of a mountain evaporate, the vegetation at the mountain's base is nourished by the light rain and mist. Since the mountain represents established strength and the lake more modest power, this hexagram represents the decrease of resources in the less privileged sector of society, and the consequent benefit to the more powerful.

When this inequitable sharing of wealth occurs in a community, instability is increased, and contributes to circumstances where loss and restraint will be felt at every social level. A nation in which the gulf between the rich and poor is too broad is like a building in which weakened and neglected foundations are expected to bear the weight of the opulently zfurnished upper levels. If this situation is permitted to go unchecked, the question is not whether the structure will collapse, but when.

Sun advises us that, to rebalance extremes of inequality, self-discipline and frugality are required. The matter is too complex to be corrected rapidly, and so we must be on our guard against impatience and resentment. Indulging in such emotions will only make the process more difficult. On a personal level, Sun may alert us to imbalances in our own spending, saving and sharing. A particular activity may be diminishing the funds we should be using to support our lifestyle.

GUIDANCE FROM HEXAGRAM 41	
General	When resources are unjustly apportioned, instability results
Love	Focus on nourishing the ground level of your relationship—go back to the basics
Business	Be frugal with your money—redirect your resources to fundamental operations
Lifestyle	Do not be impatient or resentful about redirecting your energies or finances to the more basic concerns

Hexagram 42
I (Increase)

I is formed by Wind over Thunder. Just as sound travels further when carried by a strong wind, the hexagram embodies an increase in the already invigorating qualities that the I Ching associates with thunder.

Hexagram 41 warns of the imbalances caused when the wealthy drain the resources of the poor. I describes the very opposite: the great stabilizing force that results from a conscientious attempt to reduce inequality. The wealthy will initially experience a loss, but will reap long-term benefits as the community is strengthened and the economy invigorated. Greed and exploitation despoil the very fields from which the wealthy derive their riches. Generosity ensures continued growth.

If a nation or community is to succeed in great enterprises, it must eliminate causes of mutual resentment and encourage the goodwill of the people toward those who lead them. This is unlikely to occur in the absence of an equitable distribution of wealth. When, however, such an arrangement does prevail, the fullest advantage must be taken of it. This is a time for further advancement rather than celebration. Like all conditions, this will be impermanent, but if we swiftly and resolutely capitalize on these auspicious circumstances, much of their benefit can be preserved.

While largely concerned with material gain, I also reminds us to learn from and conserve the spirit of this time. The lessons of compassion and self-sacrifice to the common good will not fail us.

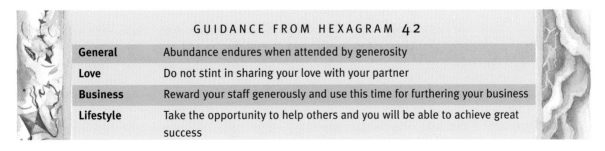

GUIDANCE FROM HEXAGRAM 42	
General	Abundance endures when attended by generosity
Love	Do not stint in sharing your love with your partner
Business	Reward your staff generously and use this time for furthering your business
Lifestyle	Take the opportunity to help others and you will be able to achieve great success

Hexagram 43
Kuai (Breakthrough)

Kuai is formed by the trigrams Lake over Heaven. When the entire contents of a lake have evaporated and ascended to the heavens, a downpour is inevitable. The clouds will not be able to bear their heavy load for long. Kuai likens this situation to individuals who, with no regard for the well-being of others, hoard their wealth or amass power. Eventually their hold on the situation will weaken, and all that they have gathered will slip from them.

Kuai indicates that, once a breakthrough of this kind occurs, we must act without hesitation to take advantage of the situation. However, although this release of accumulated energy is potentially liberating for us, like a torrential downpour it may be fraught with danger. We must be careful not to allow negative forces to regain the upper hand.

One of the dangers of which Kuai warns us is that of adopting our opponents' unethical tactics in our haste to effect change. The ends do not justify the means. Rather, means determine the ends. If we combat dishonor with dishonor, an honorable outcome will be impossible. Likewise, violence cannot give birth to lasting peace.

If our victory is achieved through brutal or underhand means, we will incur reprisals from our enemies and the mistrust of our friends. Kuai reminds us that it is more effective to challenge negativity with a positive alternative than to attempt to overpower it through force. Ideally, we should use the time preceding a breakthrough to determine more acceptable strategies.

GUIDANCE FROM HEXAGRAM 43

General	Be ready to act when the unscrupulous reveal their weakness
Love	A breakthrough will occur; it must be handled in an honorable way
Business	When an opportunity arises, use only positive strategies to achieve a breakthrough
Lifestyle	A liberating breakthrough must be approached ethically

Hexagram 44
Kou (Coming to Meet)

Kou is formed by Heaven over Wind. This image suggests the dispersal throughout the land, by the winds, of instruction in honorable and positive behavior (the ways of Heaven). It also carries a warning.

This hexagram follows on from hexagram 43, which addresses the manner in which a corrupt power can weaken. Kou, in contrast, is concerned with how virtue may be undermined. This reversal is reflected in the forms of the two trigrams. The topmost line of Kuai is yin, while all the other lines are yang, symbolizing weakness above being brought down by strength from below. In Kou the sole yin line is at the bottom, suggesting that once a new positive order has been established negative influences will immediately begin to try to sabotage it. To stress this, hexagram 43 is also associated with the Summer Solstice, the longest day of the year—the last day before daylight again begins to diminish. Just as the lessening of the light is almost imperceptible at first, so will the return of unworthy individuals or behavior commence in small and relatively harmless ways. We are warned not to underestimate how quickly these problems may gather momentum if we leave them unchecked.

The hexagram's title, "Coming to Meet," suggests the state where a virtuous person is tempted to meet with a dangerously beguiling individual who will begin to sow the seeds of corruption. If we become tainted by such contact, we must acknowledge our own fault in agreeing to the encounter.

GUIDANCE FROM HEXAGRAM 44

General	Pernicious influences must be resisted the moment you sense their presence
Love	Do not allow any harmful influences to affect your relationship
Business	Take the time to shield your business from corruption and unethical practices—these will harm you immeasurably
Lifestyle	Keep clear of any unscrupulous people or immoral suggestions

Hexagram 45
Ts'ui (Gathering Together)

Ts'ui is formed by the Lake trigram over the Earth trigram. When a lake gathers in so much water that it threatens to flood the surrounding land, it also encourages the community to gather in order to moderate the danger.

In this image, the floodwaters represent the dangers that accompany the gathering together of a large group of people. The crowd congregating to minimize the threat symbolizes the ways in which order and stability fortify a community.

The I Ching frequently stresses the immense power of a group of people that is unified by a shared sense of purpose. Ts'ui, however, reminds us that in any large assembly there will be those uninterested in the common good; in their ignorance and arrogance, such people consider themselves to be predators attracted by a large herd of unsuspecting and gentler beasts. Theft, swindling, exploitation and assault will inevitably thrive in any place where large numbers of people gather. A celebrating crowd may also endanger individuals through its very exuberance.

Enlightened and conscientious leadership is required if a community's worthiest aspects are to be fostered and its weaknesses controlled and corrected. Like many hexagrams that discuss the subject, Ts'ui stresses that leadership should be based on the encouragement of mutual respect and goodwill. This hexagram accentuates in particular the leader's need for vigilance and foresight.

GUIDANCE FROM HEXAGRAM 45

General	Social harmony is a prerequisite for prosperity
Love	Your relationship will thrive if both partners work harmoniously toward a common goal
Business	A large project must be handled in a respectful way
Lifestyle	If you are involved with a large group, focus on achieving the common goal with integrity and care

Hexagram 46
Sheng (Pushing Upward)

Sheng is formed by the Earth trigram over the Wind trigram. The I Ching relates wind to wood, and so Sheng is suggestive of the quiet, steady growth of a sapling as it pushes up through the nourishing soil in Spring. The sapling, a fruit tree, then rises above the earth, but remains dependent upon its deeply buried roots for nutrition and stability.

If kept from harm the fruit tree will bring forth blossoms and later its fruit, but it cannot be hurried in its growth. Sheng likewise announces a time of gradual but continuous growth in our enterprises.

Unlike the effortless progress associated with hexagram 35, achieving advancement at this time will take some willpower. The burgeoning seed needs to force its way through obstacles before it breaks the surface of the earth. This type of growth, however, is not forced. It develops naturally and is untroubled by doubts and errors.

Although expansion is assured, it will not necessarily be as rapid as we may like. We must resist impulsiveness and impatience, which are typically born of a lack of confidence in our ability to succeed. We will not help the growth of a seed by uncovering it periodically to check on its progress, nor will we attempt to unfold a bud to see its flower sooner. The trust we have in these natural processes, Sheng assures us, is also appropriate to our projects and ambitions at this auspicious time. This is not to say that we can rest from our labors. The new plant grows strong only through perseverance.

GUIDANCE FROM HEXAGRAM 46

General	The blossoms of Spring must be permitted to unfold in their own time
Love	Your relationship will prosper through patience and quiet nurturing
Business	Focus on the success of your business and the rewards will come to fruition
Lifestyle	Be confident in the success of your plans—keep working on them

Hexagram 47

K'un (Exhaustion)

K'un consists of the trigrams Lake above Water. This suggests a lakebed from which all the water has poured away downhill. The image symbolizes a situation in which continuous affliction has depleted our vitality, faith and enthusiasm.

Since these qualities are among the most essential to us in our endeavors, the condition described by this hexagram is particularly dangerous. Other hexagrams describing difficult times show that adversity can concentrate our efforts and determination. This hexagram shows that despair can sometimes undermine even our desire for success.

Since we are generally unreceptive to advice in this state, K'un observes that our wisest course is to prepare for such eventualities well in advance, strengthening our resistance to self-pity before negative situations occur. A sufferer of migraines does not make his or her assessment of life while suffering a severe headache.

We should also consider exhaustion and depression as passing conditions, not as indications of life as it truly is. When we remind ourselves that despondency has physical as well as emotional causes and is a temporary illness only, its treatment becomes obvious. We should allow ourselves rest and well-balanced nutrition. We should also cultivate a positive mental attitude—this has been proven to be a major factor in many forms of healing. Pessimism is a symptom of exhaustion, just as sneezing is of hay fever, and should be treated with no more seriousness. As our strength and sense of purpose return, so will our outlook be renewed.

GUIDANCE FROM HEXAGRAM 47

General	A sense of purpose is the most valuable asset
Love	Do not fall into despair or depression about your relationship—take time to rejuvenate it
Business	Do not make any important decisions concerning your business at this time
Lifestyle	Take time to rest and recuperate, focusing on improving your diet

Hexagram 48
Ching (The Well)

Ching comprises the trigrams Water over Wind. In the I Ching, the Wind trigram is associated with the element of wood, suggesting the wooden poles that were traditionally used for lowering ceramic bowls into wells to gather drinking water. This symbolism also reflects the way in which the wooden trunk of a tree draws moisture from the earth to nourish the plant.

A community without pure water could not survive, so the image of the well suggests the necessities for a community's survival. The water is associated with the nutrition of the spirit. The appearance of the community's dwelling place may alter throughout the centuries, but the necessity for the well will remain unchanged. When the spirit thirsts it must reach beyond the superficialities of the world to that which lies beneath.

The water may variously represent love, religious or spiritual revelations, abiding social order or education, depending on the needs of the individual and the community. Regardless of what is needed at any given time, we are reminded that when a well is allowed to become tainted or if we damage our means of drawing sustenance, we will be unable to slake the thirst we are seeking to remedy. We must ensure that our access to uncontaminated sources of refreshment, physical or spiritual, are carefully maintained. This will often prove an antidote for the exhaustion described in hexagram 47.

Ching also emphasizes our duty to provide this sustenance of the soul for those who are unable to do so themselves. By ensuring that this nourishment is available to all, we will contribute enormously to the stability and contentment of the community.

GUIDANCE FROM HEXAGRAM 48

General	Although human culture changes, there is constancy in the needs of the spirit
Love	Remember to nourish the soul in order to sustain your relationship
Business	Attempt to cater for the basic or constant needs of humanity rather than following fads
Lifestyle	Nurture your spirit and make sure your basic needs are well provided for

Ko (Revolution)

Ko is formed by the placement of Lake over Fire. This unnatural ordering of elements suggests a dramatic conflict in nature. The rising subterranean heat will threaten the lake with evaporation, while the sinking waters of the lake will attempt to cool or quench the fire.

The I Ching emphasizes that such dynamic oppositions are the essence of life, reflected in the changing of night into day, winter into summer and so on. In this case, however, the conflict is extreme. Ko predicts a time of transformation radical enough to be compared to a political revolution.

It is important not to assume that all such changes must be effected swiftly. Although the initial success of many revolutions is determined by fast, decisive action, those not founded on a solid base of preparation are just as quickly reversed or undermined by weaknesses within. Revolutionary battles have been won many times by people with no idea about what to do once they have triumphed.

Ko reminds us that the disruptions caused by radical change demand that we undertake it only when strictly necessary, and then only after the meticulous planning of our responses to every eventuality. Once our course of action is clear, we must still await the most advantageous time for action. When this time comes, we must resist acting impetuously. Maintaining a good sense of timing is imperative.

GUIDANCE FROM HEXAGRAM 49

General	Radical change must be justified by necessity and guided by clarity of intention
Love	You may need to do something radical concerning your relationship, but plan first for every eventuality
Business	For optimal benefit, choose wisely your moment for effecting radical change
Lifestyle	Meditate on how to take advantage of this time of change so you can achieve self-transformation

Hexagram 50
Ting (The Cauldron)

Ting is formed by the placement of Fire over Wind. Since Wind is also related to wood in the I Ching, Ting evokes the image of the flames rising from a well-ventilated campfire.

The purpose of such a fire is to provide comfort and to prepare food, both of which ideas are furthered by the hexagram's suggestion of the traditional bronze cooking vessel for which the hexagram was named. Four yang lines represent the body and lid of the traditional Chinese ting, while the yin lines suggest its legs and handles.

Like hexagram 48, which relates to the waters of a village well, Ting is concerned with the provision of a community's necessities of life, both physical and spiritual. The simplicity of the well and the drinking water, however, is replaced here by the sophistication of the elegant cauldron and complex meals. Cooking is not merely a matter of supplying our nutrients. It is a transformative art, symbolizing all of the achievements of a harmonious culture. The sharing of a carefully prepared meal is also one of the most commonly practiced rituals for binding communities together.

Accordingly, Ting indicates a time of conviviality and artistry and a celebration of the more civilizing and enriching aspects of life. It also stresses that we must attend to spiritual as well as worldly needs. The ting was traditionally the vessel use for presenting offerings to departed ancestors, deities and other spiritual powers.

GUIDANCE FROM HEXAGRAM 50

General	A harmonious life is based on the nourishment of body, mind and spirit
Love	Enjoy the harmonious aspects of your relationship—this will deepen your bonds
Business	Focus on business that will help transform your affairs and add sophistication to your dealings
Lifestyle	Host a dinner for some of those most important to you to strengthen the relationships between everyone attending

Hevagram 51
Chen (The Arousing)

The trigrams forming Chen are Thunder over Thunder. In the I Ching thunder generally represents the power to invigorate and revitalize us. In this hexagram, however, it is present in increased intensity, and as such heralds situations that may alarm or even terrify us for a time. Thunder will, however, result in improved conditions if we react wisely to its influence.

An individual in extreme fear will often attempt to bargain with the higher powers for deliverance, promising to lead a better life in exchange. Chen jolts us out of complacency, encouraging us to examine our lives for errors, unkindness and unworthiness. If we approach the examination conscientiously, we will come through this testing time stronger and wiser. Often, however, we will forget our promises to improve our ways only moments after the danger has passed. If we slide back into destructive habits after the storm, we will have gained nothing from it. We must value the changes that come when we confront our fears. Courage is not the lack of fear, but the willingness to face it. By focusing on the advantages we can win through this process, we will lessen our dread and fortify our resolve.

The greater our concerns during a wild storm, the more we will relish normal existence once the storm has passed. This hexagram advises us on how to act after a crisis. We should blend our increased appreciation for life with a sense of achievement at having faced up to fear—then we will be amply rewarded for our efforts.

GUIDANCE FROM HEXAGRAM 51	
General	If you wish the air to be cleared, you should not object to the storm
Love	Rise to the challenge of your relationship and examine your behavior to see if destructive habits can be eradicated
Business	Your business may be facing an alarming setback, but you will be able to prevail if you strengthen your resolve
Lifestyle	Learn to face your fears—this will help you to become a stronger person

Hexagram 52
Ken (Keeping Still)

Ken comprises the trigrams Mountain over Mountain. In hexagram 51 the doubling of the invigorating influence of thunder relates to energetic change, but Ken is the epitome of stillness and tranquillity.

In the philosophy of the I Ching, all action, speech and thought require emptiness as a precondition. As a cup that is not hollow cannot be filled, so is a full and cluttered mind unable to hold new thoughts. Stillness precedes activity, just as restful sleep must precede an effective day's work.

In many cultures, mountaintops are considered places of meditative retreat. Ken counsels us to withdraw for a time from worldly activities so that we can approach them thereafter with renewed clarity and strength. We are reminded, however, that there is a world of difference between simply resting and true meditation. Cultivating inner stillness requires a great deal of patience, persistence and self-discipline. Our minds are unaccustomed to abandoning activity and chatter, and need to be trained.

It is no easy task to free our minds of anxieties and scheming, but the more we can do so, the more objectively and clearly we will see the circumstances of our lives when we return to activity. Our misapprehensions and delusions are held in place by continuous internal reiteration, trapping us. When we are able to switch off these mental tape loops, we will regain our ability to think independently.

GUIDANCE FROM HEXAGRAM 52	
General	All effective action must be born out of stillness
Love	Let go of preconceptions in order to see the situation clearly
Business	Remember to clear your mind of clutter before making an important business decision
Lifestyle	Learn the skill of meditation or other techniques to help you achieve periods with a "still" mind

Hexagram 53
Chien (Gradual Progress)

Chien is constructed by the trigrams Wind over Mountain. Because of Wind's association with wood in the I Ching, this hexagram is related to the image of a tree growing on a windswept mountaintop. Unlike one that grows in a lush, sheltered environment, this tree must grow slowly, extending its roots deeply into the ground and developing a trunk powerful enough to withstand the elements.

This hexagram therefore describes a period in which we should cultivate patience, and focus on gradual development in all areas of life—from business or artistic projects to relationships. There is no question that we will not gain ground—we will move forward without haste. This state should not give rise to anxiety or restlessness; instead it should be seen as an opportunity to make sure we are attending to every necessary particular. A rider makes better time than a walker, but will learn much less of the land between the origin and the destination.

Chien offers, as an example of this steady advancement, the formalities that precede a wedding. These may seem cumbersome, but when they are not observed we may lose the opportunity for many of the complex readjustments that the blending of the bride's and groom's families require. A rushed wedding with little sense of occasion is often followed by disappointment and a lack of familial support.

The time spent on meticulous attention to detail and the diligent nurturing of our enterprises and relationships will, Chien assures us, be greatly rewarded in the near future.

GUIDANCE FROM HEXAGRAM 53

General	When advancement is steady and patient, you can perfect every detail
Love	Make unhurried and steady progress with deepening your relationship
Business	Take the time to focus on the details of your business
Lifestyle	In order to appreciate the fullness of your life, focus on its particulars

Hexagram 54
Kuei Mei (The Marrying Maiden)

Kuei Mei comprises the trigrams Thunder over Lake. The image of this hexagram is of the waters of the lake rippling under the influence of the thunder high above. As the Lake trigram is associated with the youngest daughter of the family, this image is associated with the way in which the young and inexperienced may fall prey to infatuation.

The hexagram's title elaborates upon this, suggesting a young woman who—not heeding the warning of hexagram 53—has married in haste someone with whom no true connection is possible. As a result of this ill-advised union, she now finds herself alienated from her family and in a relationship with one who offers her little attention, respect or affection. Faced with a situation with little hope, she acknowledges that her maidenhood is over. Spring has abruptly transformed into Fall.

One of the most challenging hexagrams, Kuei Mei offers a caution. It reminds us that when major errors in judgment lead us into complex situations we should not make matters worse with further impetuous behavior. To seek remedies, we must proceed slowly and with great diplomacy and forbearance.

We are also counseled against anger and self-pity. Like all situations described in the I Ching, the current one will eventually pass, and a degree of resignation and perspective will strengthen us enormously. The autumnal mood Kuei Mei invokes should prepare us to endure the coming Winter with fortitude, and with confidence that Spring will come in its turn.

GUIDANCE FROM HEXAGRAM 54	
General	Disappointment is best cured by a sense of perspective
Love	Be careful to see the difference between infatuation and true love
Business	Be aware of impetuous business decisions
Lifestyle	If faced with a complex situation, focus on progressing slowly and cautiously

Hexagram 55
Feng (Abundance)

Feng is formed by the arrangement of Thunder over Fire. This suggests the brilliance and beauty of lightning flashing from storm clouds toward the earth. As the thunderstorm in the I Ching represents an invigorating, expansive and liberating force, Feng represents a period of spectacular success and great abundance.

Just as a magnificent storm cannot sustain itself indefinitely, this period of triumph will prove as transitory as all other conditions described in the I Ching. Feng advises us to bear this in mind, but not to feel dispirited by the decline that must follow. There is no point in feeling unhappy at noon at the thought of the sun's descent. This time of brightness should be appreciated, and the remaining hours of daylight used to provide for the hours of night. If we take advantage of these auspicious conditions wisely, their benefits will last well into the future.

If, however, we become lazy, complacent or self-indulgent in our success, we may indeed have cause for regret before long. These are the errors we are inclined to make when dazzled by our achievements, and forgetful of the I Ching's lesson that all circumstances must change.

It is appropriate to celebrate personal and communal victories with family, friends and well-wishers, but we need to remain wary of making foolish decisions in the midst of such pleasurable distractions. Major success does not come easily or often enough to most of us to be treated lightly or irresponsibly when it passes our way.

GUIDANCE FROM HEXAGRAM 55	
General	Be mindful, even at the peak of success, of providing for the future
Love	Celebrate the success of your relationship
Business	Make further plans even as you celebrate a major business success
Lifestyle	This is a period of great triumph in your endeavors—make the most of your success for lasting benefits

Hexagram 56
Lu (The Wanderer)

Lu comprises the trigrams Fire over Mountain. The image associated with this combination is of a wildfire blazing across a mountaintop. Since there is a finite amount of combustible vegetation on the mountain, the fire will move rapidly in search of more fuel to sustain it.

This symbol represents the need for travel that periodically comes upon us, in order to provide our minds, hearts or spirits with something we are lacking in our lives. This lack may result from the depletion of something we have previously had in abundance, or it may concern aspects of life we have not yet experienced. Either way, Lu encourages us to commence our quest.

The hexagram also reminds us of the hazards of the road. Once we have journeyed beyond our familiar habitat, our relative ignorance can make us vulnerable to deception and confusion, and to hostility caused by our inadvertent discourtesy. We must remain attentive to variations in customs and beliefs; we must treat all those we meet with deference and delicacy, while ensuring that our tact does not tip over into blatant insincerity.

Lu cautions us in other matters too. Certain hexagrams (notably hexagram 33) advise travel as a means of eluding danger. Lu, however, recommends journeying toward knowledge rather than fleeing from difficulties. We are advised to cultivate self-awareness, so that we will know when we are embarking upon travel to avoid issues we would do better to confront.

GUIDANCE FROM HEXAGRAM 56

General	You will travel best when the journey is a quest rather than an escape
Love	Travel will help provide your heart with something you are lacking in your relationship, but do not use it as an escape
Business	Travel is advised to provide the business with something it is lacking—use tact and courtesy to help you in your journey
Lifestyle	Travel is suggested as a way to gain knowledge in a particular area

Hexagram 57
Sun (The Gentle)

Sun is formed by the trigrams Wind over Wind. Unable to be seen or grasped, the wind can nevertheless cause great changes in the environment. The doubling of the trigram in Sun emphasizes gentle persistence, not only in strength but also in direction. A constantly changing wind will dissipate its power, but when it blows predominantly from a single direction it will shape the entire landscape.

Accordingly, hexagram 57 encourages us to follow this example in our current projects, and to act gently but unceasingly rather than suddenly and aggressively. There are times (such as those discussed in hexagram 49) when swift, decisive action is called for. Sun reminds us, though, that such action runs the risk of consolidating and empowering the forces that oppose us. We will strengthen our position by minimizing resistance, and this will be achieved more enduringly through persuasion and the creation of trust than through coercion and punishment.

Just as the breeze gently penetrates obstacles, Sun advises us to see that our ideas are given ample opportunity to permeate the consciousness of those from whom we seek support. If these ideas and strategies are misunderstood or fail to convince at the outset, we must patiently reiterate and expand upon them until their merit is absorbed. Only then will our instructions be agreed to without the need for force. Like the wind, we must adapt our behavior to the nature of the obstructions we encounter. We must remain humble and approachable without erring toward docility. Gentleness must not become weakness.

GUIDANCE FROM HEXAGRAM 57

General	Rapid change may be effected by force, but enduring change is accomplished by gentle persistence
Love	Develop trust in your relationship through patient and thorough action
Business	Use gentle persuasion to further your business plans
Lifestyle	Gentle persistence will help you achieve your plans

Hexagram 58
Tui (Joy)

Tui comprises the trigrams Lake over Lake. This doubling up of the trigram suggests an elevated lake in the mountains, contributing water to a smaller lake on the plains that would otherwise be in danger of depletion. Since the Lake trigram in the I Ching is associated with joy, the higher lake, fed by springs and mountain mists, becomes a symbol for the nurturing, happiness and encouragement we receive from people who inspire us, and from situations in which all seems possible.

The climate Tui describes is one in which the community is united by infectious buoyancy. Anxiety and disharmony are banished by a sense of achievement and triumph that seems to promise even greater things.

Of all forms of motivation, the possibility of attaining true bliss is the most powerful. Bliss in this sense means a quality of elation that touches all aspects of our being. Sensual pleasures, intellectual stimulation and emotional contentment gratify only parts of our consciousness, whereas bliss enflames the entire being. Tui pertains to conditions that give us a taste of this holistic delight and hold out the promise of more to come.

We should not, however, allow ourselves to become intoxicated by this communal exuberance. Revelry will only distract us from capitalizing on this auspicious time. Further advancement is possible if we are inspired by our successes, but neither besotted with or reliant upon them. More obstacles lie ahead, but these will be mastered if we are guided equally by joy and by wisdom.

GUIDANCE FROM HEXAGRAM 58

General	Nothing inspires the human spirit more than the achievability of bliss
Love	You will experience great joy in your relationship
Business	Capitalize on your success—all things are now possible
Lifestyle	Enjoy the feeling of bliss in your life and continue advancing fueled by the inspiration of your current successes

Hexagram 59
Huan (Dispersion)

Huan is formed by the trigrams Wind over Water. When a stream is cluttered with fallen leaves it may become dammed, possibly to the point of stagnation. In such circumstances, a strong breeze may help to clear the debris, allowing the waters to flow more freely. Similarly, the warm winds of Spring will help to dissolve the ice covering a pond.

Accordingly, this hexagram suggests the forces that remove barriers to unity, fluidity and progress. There may be a degree of disruption in our lives when this process is required. This is reflected in the fact that the two elements of Wind and Water can have only limited inter-action. The wind does not penetrate the water, but causes effects on its surface only. This also emphasizes that outside forces, such as mediators and arbiters, may be necessary to resolve the conflicts alienating members of a family, team or community.

Just as a blocked watercourse may require the assistance of a powerful wind to liberate it, so too do social obstacles often need to be tackled strenuously. Huan alerts us, however, to the dangers associated with waves whipped up by too wild a wind. As far as possible we must contain damage to aspects of the relationship not directly related to the cause of the conflict or stalemate.

Since the I Ching associates Wind with Wood, Huan takes on the image of a boat, further symbolizing the communication and cooperation we should be striving for. Where a body of water divides individuals, we must find ways in which they may be united.

GUIDANCE FROM HEXAGRAM 59

General	You will advance your aims by working to eliminate the causes of disharmony
Love	Strengthen communication in order to remove barriers to your union
Business	Business progress will be achieved again by persistent communication
Lifestyle	To lighten your current concerns, move persistently toward unity and integration

Hexagram 60

Chieh (Limitation)

The two trigrams forming Chieh are Water over Lake. This suggests heavy rain above a lake, or excessive run-off from waters in the highlands. Although the lake requires replenishment, too much, such as the overflow of water encountered in hexagram 28, will have disruptive consequences.

This symbol represents our need for practical limitation in our lives. A lake is defined by its form and volume. Its dimensions will expand and contract throughout time within certain parameters, but it remains, like ourselves, a finite container able to bear only a fraction of an immeasurably larger resource. Just as water exists in quantities far greater than the capacity of a single lake, so do the complexities of the universe and the possibilities of human life lie far beyond any individual's ability to assimilate them all. When we attempt too much, we threaten our sense of identity.

This does not mean that we are incapable of growth. We must simply grow at the appropriate rate. A lake may change its shape and size gradually over many decades and still be considered the same body of water by the local residents. Similarly, we can develop and change advantageously when we do not attempt to do so at a precipitant rate.

In practical terms, Chieh advises moderation. Overindulgence and spending beyond our means are clearly not conducive to our long-term happiness. We must be careful, though, to make balance rather than self-denial our aim. While an overfed lake creates dangerous floods, a starved lake is reduced to mud.

GUIDANCE FROM HEXAGRAM 60

General	Although our potential is limitless, our capabilities at any given time are not
Love	Do not move quickly toward an intense relationship, but start slowly building a strong and lasting friendship
Business	Do not overreach yourself in business—focus on quality rather than quantity
Lifestyle	Concentrate on slowly achieving long-term happiness

Hexagram 61
Chung Fu (Inner Truth)

Chung Fu is formed by the trigrams Wind over Lake. Ripples on the surface of the lake indicate the invisible force of the breeze. This image suggests the way thought influences behavior, and the way the inner, spiritual world influences external reality.

To perceive that which the eyes cannot register, we must learn to see with the heart. The hexagram's shape, with a hollow area at the center of the otherwise solid looking form, is likened by the I Ching to the openness of the heart in a perceptive individual.

In order to communicate and cooperate well with others, we must be able to comprehend their natures. To do so, we must banish preconceptions, prejudice and any other factors that decrease receptivity. In their place, we must cultivate compassion. This is suggested by another interpretation of Chung Fu's shape: a representation of two mouths meeting in a kiss as the two trigrams mirror each other.

Once we have deepened our understanding of how others think, feel and view their lives, we can work to establish their trust. We should only do so, however, with sincerity and a desire for mutual benefit. Manipulating people for our own gain may bring temporary advantages, but once our deception has been recognized this progress may be undone by the justifiable resentment that hypocrisy engenders. We must use the unseen power of our ideas and words gently, honestly and honorably if we wish to effect lasting change in the visible world.

GUIDANCE FROM HEXAGRAM 61

General	To influence others deeply, take the time to understand them deeply
Love	Take the time to understand your partner thoroughly in order to gain trust
Business	Sincere and straightforward communication will aid a business partnership immeasurably
Lifestyle	Cultivate compassion and a deep understanding of the people who are affecting your life

Hexagram 62
Hsaio Kuo (The Preponderance of the Small)

Hsaio Kuo is formed by the trigrams Thunder over Mountain. As we ascend a mountain, we hear the commanding sound of the thunder above. However, when we reach the peak and hear its enthusiastic call to action at close range, there is nowhere for us to go but downward.

This situation symbolizes the need to refrain temporarily from trying to achieve great victories, and the need to return to more mundane matters. This should not discourage us; rather, we should approach the smaller, humbler projects to which we are directed with all the passion and commitment that we would usually apply to major challenges.

In terms of the distribution of yin and yang lines, this hexagram is the opposite of hexagram 28 (called "The Preponderance of the Great"), which warns of the weakening of a massive structure. Instead of the downfall of the great, Hsaio Kuo speaks of strength proceeding from the small. This is consequently a time to concentrate on details rather than on overly ambitious projects. The I Ching advises us that our appropriate course at this time is to be like a bird in a storm that flies down to the security of her nest rather than upward to challenge the elements.

In hexagram 9, such attention to small matters is advised as a way in which to use our time while awaiting more favorable circumstances. Hsaio Kuo, in contrast, tells us that it is through this very attention to minutiae that progress can be made.

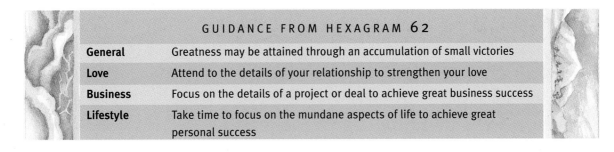

GUIDANCE FROM HEXAGRAM 62	
General	Greatness may be attained through an accumulation of small victories
Love	Attend to the details of your relationship to strengthen your love
Business	Focus on the details of a project or deal to achieve great business success
Lifestyle	Take time to focus on the mundane aspects of life to achieve great personal success

Hexagram 63

Chi Chi (After Completion)

Chi Chi comprises the trigrams Water over Fire. The form of the hexagram denotes the achievement of perfect order. The trigrams are each other's opposites, and the lines alternate between yin and yang, each being in its appropriate place with regard to strength and weakness—the yang being in the strong positions and the yin in the weak. The hexagram is therefore representative of successful conclusion.

The image associated with Chi Chi is that of a kettle of water suspended above a cooking fire. Although this reflects the appropriate placement of the elements for productive interaction, we are reminded that this harmony must be carefully tended. If our attention wanders, the fire may rise too high and boil the kettle dry, or the water may overflow to extinguish the flames. Through this imagery, Chi Chi reminds us that change continues even at the moment of our triumph, and that we must be on the alert for eventualities that will undermine the advantages we have won. We should certainly take time to celebrate our success, since a joyless victory is barely worth winning. We must not, however, fall into complacency, arrogance or self-indulgence. If our achievement is to endure, we must immediately take pains to consolidate it.

It is important to see the conclusion of any chapter of our lives—successful or otherwise—as the commencement of another. The greatest victory may be rapidly eroded, and the greatest disaster the foundation of a future profit. When we remain mindful that all conditions are temporary, we will increase our control of where those changes will take us.

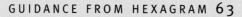

GUIDANCE FROM HEXAGRAM 63

General	As every ending is a beginning, every triumph inaugurates new challenges
Love	You will move toward a deeper phase of your relationship
Business	Consolidate your business success and celebrate your achievements
Lifestyle	Celebrate your success and plan for sustaining a new phase of your life

Hexagram 64
Wei Chi (Before Completion)

Wei Chi is formed by Fire over Water. Fire, which rises up, and water, which descends, do not interrelate. This suggests that the ideal situation has almost been achieved, but there is still work to be done. At a casual glance, Wei Chi looks so similar to hexagram 63. Also consisting of alternating yin and yang lines and opposite trigrams, hexagram 63 represents completion. In Wei Chi, however, the yang lines are in the weak positions and the yin in the strong. The correct internal equilibrium has not yet been established.

Endings are invariably dangerous times, since we are often tempted to hasten toward the finish line, neglecting the remaining details; yet these may prove to be our downfall. We cannot underestimate the negligence that the nearness of victory can engender. We are counseled not to be like a fox in Winter who, anxious to complete his journey across a partially frozen stream, misjudges his final leap to safety and is rewarded by the immersion of his tail in the freezing water. For this reason the hexagram is also known as "The River Not Yet Crossed."

Impatience and premature pride in our performance often present challenges in such circumstances, but they must be overcome. If we can remain alert to danger and focused on the tasks at hand, Wei Chi assures us that a successful conclusion to our efforts can be attained.

GUIDANCE FROM HEXAGRAM 64

General	We must be especially vigilant during our final approach to success
Love	Be careful not to remove your full attention from your goal—do not get distracted
Business	Do not move your focus away from achieving completion of your goals
Lifestyle	Concentrate on not allowing impatience or pride to get in the way of your success

Glossary

chi: See qi

elements: There are five elements underlying Chinese Taoist philosophy: Metal, Water, Wood, Fire, and Earth. It is believed that everything on earth, including human beings, is made up of a combination of these elements.

hexagram: A set of six broken (yin) and unbroken (yang) lines, constructed in response to a question put to the I Ching. A hexagram is made up of two trigrams. The lower trigram indicates the cause of a situation and the upper the surface appearances of the issue. There are 64 hexagrams in the I Ching, representing 64 spiritual principles.

I Ching: Translated variously as the "Book of Changes" or the "Classic of Change," this is perhaps the oldest writing on philosophy, cosmology, divination and self-transformation in Chinese civilization.

ki: See qi

qi: Also known as chi or ki, an invisible but powerful energy that flows around and within everything in the universe. It is created and stimulated by the balance of two extreme forms of energy, yin (feminine) and yang (masculine). There are many levels of qi, such as heaven qi, earth qi and human qi, and more intimate levels, such as personal qi, which reflects the energy that moves through your body, thoughts, emotions and personality. Every organ in your body has its particular quality of qi; for example, there is a kidney qi, a heart qi, and a liver qi.

san cai: The "Three Treasures," or the Chinese trinity of Heaven, Earth and humanity. The upper line of the trigram represents Heaven, the bottom line Earth, and the middle line humanity. Also known as the trinity principle of cosmic unity.

Taoism: Along with Confucianism and Buddhism, one of the three great philosophies of China. Tao can be translated as "path." The I Ching contains a wealth of Taoist knowledge, including the Taoist notions of "oneness" and that everything in the universe is part of a "continuum."

trigram: Three-line figures forming the hexagrams. There are eight trigrams, believed to unveil the heavenly processes in nature and to aid in the understanding of the character of everything—they could be used to depict and explain the existence of all physical, psychological, natural and social manifestations. In a hexagram, the lower trigram indicates the cause of the situation and the upper indicates the surface appearances of the issue.

yin and yang: The two great primordial forces of nature. According to Chinese philosophy, everything was created through the interaction of these forces. They govern the cycle of birth, growth and decay of all things material, mental and spiritual. Yin and yang are not precisely defined, but at their most basic level yin corresponds with female, passive energy and flexibility, and yang with male, active energy and firmness of will.

Further reading

Blofeld, J., *I Ching: The Book of Changes*, Mandala Books (Unwin), London, 1980 reprint.

Lawler, J., *Dragon Insights: A Simple Approach to the I Ching*, Simon & Schuster, Sydney, 2001.

Legge, J., *I Ching: Book of Changes* (trans.), Gramercy Books, New York, 1996.

Schoenholtz, L., *New Directions in the I Ching: The Yellow River Legacy*, University Books Inc., Secaucus, New Jersey, 1974.

Toropov, B., *I Ching for Beginners*, Writers and Readers Publishing Inc., New York, 1996.

Tsu, Lao, *Tao Te Ching*, Penguin, London, 1983 reprint.

Watts, A., *Tao: The Watercourse Way*, Penguin, New York, 1981 reprint.

Wilhelm, R., *I Ching or Book of Changes* (trans.), Routledge & Kegan Paul, London, 1980 reprint.

The aim of I Ching practice is to bring about
balance in which celestial consciousness
guides earthly awareness to follow the
rhythm of nature.